HAPPINESS

A GUIDE TO A GOOD LIFE

HAPPINESS

ARISTOTLE FOR THE NEW CENTURY

JEAN VANIER

Translated from the French by Kathryn Spink

ARCADE PUBLISHING • NEW YORK

FIRST U.S. EDITION 2002

The author wishes to thank the publishers and copyright holders of the cited texts for permission to reproduce their material.

Originally published in Canada by House of Anansi Press Limited

Library of Congress Cataloging-in-Publication Data

Vanier, Jean, 1928–
   [Goût du bonheur. English]
   Happiness : a guide to a good life : Aristotle for the new century / Jean Vanier. —1st U.S. ed.
      p. cm.
   Translated by Kathryn Spink
   Originally published: Made for happiness. Toronto : House of Anansi Press, 2001.
   ISBN 1-55970-644-9
    1. Aristotle. 2. Ethics. 3. Happiness. I. Title.

B491.E7 V3613 2002
171'.3—dc21   2002074629

Published in the United States by Arcade Publishing, Inc., New York
Distributed by AOL Time Warner Book Group

Visit our Web site at www.arcadepub.com

10 9 8 7 6 5 4 3 2 1

EB

PRINTED IN THE UNITED STATES OF AMERICA

CONTENTS

ABBREVIATIONS

NE *Nichomachean Ethics*

EE *Eudemian Ethics,* Aristotle's first ethical treatise which is appreciably similar to the *Nichomachean Ethics*

Pol. *Politics*

Meta. *Metaphysics*

Phys. *Physics*

De Cael. *De Caelo (On the Heavens)*

Rhet. *Rhetoric*

Top. *Topics*

Poet. *Poetics*

De Part. *De Partibus Animalium (On the Parts of Animals)*

De Div. *De Divinatione per Somnum (On Prophesying by Dreams)*

NOTE

Aristotle refers exclusively to "man," and there are times when, in order to avoid making the text too heavy, I too have used the word "man" in the generic sense. In Aristotle's day, men were considered to be superior to women. Therein lies one of the shortcomings of his ethics. Today we would refer more readily and appropriately to "human beings," "people," or "men and women."

INTRODUCTION

Happiness, whatever else people may say, is the great concern of our life. A brief inquiry will easily bear this out. We would only have to ask people rushing to work, strolling about the streets, or chatting over a drink, "What are you looking for in life?" Some might say, "success at work, promotion"; others, "marriage, starting a family" or "a peaceful life without conflict," or "a salary increase, a holiday in the sun, a good time with friends." But if we were to press them further, "Why do you want to be successful, earn a salary increase, start a family, or have an enjoyable holiday?" their answer would no doubt be, "Because it would make me happy."

To be happy, to know happiness, is the great desire of every man and woman. We may differ perhaps in the means by which we attain happiness, but we all want to be happy. That is our great aspiration.

Caught up as we are in the business of living and our various activities, it is true that we do not often ask ourselves, "Why am I doing this, what am I looking for?" Yet this is the unavoidable question about the meaning of life. And as soon as we ask ourselves that question, we start to philosophize.

Why is a human being created? For what happiness? That is the question the Greek philosophers posed, the question the Jewish people asked, the question central to Jesus' message in the *Beatitudes*. It is the question that has existed in the hearts of men and women of all times, backgrounds, races, and religions. It is humanity's eternal question.

Aristotle is one of the great witnesses to this quest for happiness. His thinking was not that of an ideologue, but based on human facts and personal experience. That was what led him to propound his ethics of happiness in order to help people to look more clearly into themselves and to find their own fulfillment. He did so 2,400 years ago, but his thinking spans the centuries and is still relevant to us today.

Aristotle believes in human intelligence. He is convinced that what distinguishes human beings from animals is the capacity to think, to know and analyze reality, to make choices, to orient our lives in one direction or another. He does not accept that we are merely a collection of predestined desires or impulses. He thinks that each of us is, to a greater or lesser extent, master of our own life and destiny.

Aristotle does not, however, seek merely to reiterate moral axioms. Nor does he wish to prompt people by external means to be just, to seek the truth, and to obey laws. What he wants to do is lay the foundations of a moral science with thinking that stems from humanity's deep desires. His fundamental question is not "What ought we to do?" but "What do we really want?" His ethics are not those of law. Rather, they look closely at humanity's deepest inclinations in order to bring them to their ultimate fulfillment. Aristotle's ethics are not therefore based on an idea but on the desire for fullness of life inscribed in every human being.

Aristotle's ethics require that we work on ourselves. We might be disappointed that they do not provide us with the clear moral guidelines for action that we are seeking, or with the principles that we might expect ethics to propound. Instead Aristotle invites us to look for and discern those guidelines within ourselves. "What is your deepest desire, hidden perhaps beneath other, more superficial desires?" It is for us to work that out.

Aristotle's thinking is not without its limitations, and we shall look at those in the conclusion to this book. He is often criticized for being too comfortable with slavery and the subordination of women. In his defence, we should bear in mind that nearly two and a half millennia separate him from us. The interim years have seen the birth of Christianity, the emergence of big cities, all the discoveries of science, and an extraordinary evolution in the way in which men and women live. All this has led human beings to new discoveries about themselves and the roles of men and women. Women are no longer — as in Aristotle's day, when infant mortality was high — completely tied to the task of giving birth to children and looking after the family. Women can now more readily take their place in society, without neglecting their role as mothers in the process.

If there are deficiencies in Aristotle's thinking, there are also things of significant value. He wants to take into account the whole of human reality, not to create a system of ethics that is purely ideological. His ethics integrate the dimensions of the body and affectivity, as well as that of pleasure. They afford friendship a generous place, for Aristotle is convinced that it is impossible to be happy all on one's own: "For without friends no one would choose to live" (NE 1155a3). In a broader sense, happiness has a social or *civic* dimension. The man who wishes to be fully human cannot remain a stranger to city life.

It is this profound sense of reality and human reality that has always interested me about Aristotle, and well before the foundation of l'Arche. When I was thirteen, I entered a British naval school. It was wartime and I wanted to serve in the armed forces against the grave threat of Nazi power. I left the navy eight years later because I had begun to ask myself the question, "Is this really what I want to do with my life?" I had allowed myself to be drawn into the navy for the commendable reason of serving my country. I left the navy because of a deeper questioning: "What do I want to do with my life? What will make me a fully accomplished man?"

My departure from the navy led me to seek the meaning of life in my Christian faith, in Jesus' message of peace and his vision of humanity. I also sought answers from philosophers, and from wise men and women who were convinced of the beauty and value of human beings. That was how I came across the works of Aristotle.

And so I immersed myself in his philosophy and especially in his ethics. In 1962 I defended a doctoral thesis at the Catholic Institute in Paris on "Happiness as Principle and End of Aristotelian Ethics." My research into the basis of Aristotelian ethics brought me a great deal of light and helped me to grasp the connection between ethics, psychology, and spirituality. Psychology helps us to understand human behaviour and grasp the fears and blockages that are in us, in order to help us free ourselves of them. Spirituality is like a breath of inspiration that strengthens our motivation. Ethics help us to clarify what is a truly human act, what justice is and what the best activities are — those that render us more human and happiest. They help us better understand to what our freedom is calling us.

After my doctorate, I began teaching philosophy in Canada. Then circumstances brought me into contact with men and women with intellectual disabilities. I discovered then how divided and fragmented our societies are. On the one hand are those who are healthy and well integrated into society; on the other are those who are excluded, on its margins. As in Aristotle's day, there are still masters and slaves. I realized that peace could not prevail while no attempt was being made to span the gulf separating different cultures, different religions, and even different individuals. That was how, with the encouragement and support of Fr. Thomas Philippe, I came to found l'Arche, in order to welcome Raphael Simi and Philippe Seux, two men with mental handicaps who had been shut away in an institution. We began to live together. They were also asking themselves about the meaning of their lives and of happiness. Like me, they wanted to be happy, and their desire showed in their expressions, their cries, their tears, their violence, and their smiles. It showed in their craving for friendship too.

I was led to ask myself these questions: What do they need in order to be happy? What are they looking for? Is it just a job, a place in society, money, an independent life in an apartment? What kind of growth to maturity is possible for people who are mentally handicapped? What form does their happiness take?

Quite quickly I realized that the Gospel and Christian spirituality could not be divorced from human, philosophical, and ethical thinking. Spirituality is not disincarnate. It is rooted in what is human.

Thus this book has its origins both in my thesis, with all its weighty pages, its philosophical precision, and its analysis of Aristotle's words and texts, and in my experience of life among fragile women and men wounded by illness and rejection. Its aim is to make the wisdom of this man, Aristotle, accessible. The trails he lays can help us not only to ask worthwhile questions but also to find good points of reference.

Many people today have no religious faith. It is important to be able to communicate with them at a rational level, to reflect upon things human and on human maturity. Many of Aristotle's principles are valid for any ethics. Being human does not mean simply obeying laws that come from outside, but attaining maturity. Being human means becoming as perfectly accomplished as possible. If we do not become fully accomplished, something is lost to the whole of humanity. For Aristotle this accomplishment derives from the exercise of the most perfect activity: that of seeking the truth in all things, shunning lies and illusion, acting in accordance with justice, transcending oneself to act for the good of others in society.

The quotations from Aristotle in this book are precise and clear. Those who wish to check those translations that I have done myself, or some of the interpretations of his ethical thought, should refer to my thesis, published by Desclée de Brouwer in 1966.[1] I have for the most part made use of the English translation of Aristotle's texts by W. D. Ross,[2] except where it seemed to me that those of Terence Irwin[3] or Michael Pakulak[4] conveyed the meaning more clearly to the modern reader. Where this is the case, it is indicated with a footnote. Where I have inserted square brackets in cited passages, it is to clarify meaning or context.

HAPPINESS

CHAPTER 1

THE ETHICS OF DESIRE

As a philosopher, Aristotle is concerned with the global vision of things. He is trying, without slipping into intransigence, to devise a comprehensive philosophy that will integrate all aspects of human knowledge, and seeking how best to encompass the goals of each one, the certainties to which each can lay claim, and the methods by which we may attain them.

Aristotle began, it seems, by giving lessons in logic: How could human intelligence progress to an understanding of reality? In order to proceed methodically with this inquiry, it was necessary first to understand the instrument with which one was working. He looked next at the physical world, the sky, the animals . . . and then, at a deeper level, he proceeded to reflect on what lay beyond that world, seeking the first causes of all beings and existence, in a form of inquiry known as metaphysics.

At the same time, in the *Politics* and the *Ethics* he broached the subject of human action. He wanted to investigate what it was that enabled a human being to reach his full potential, to become accomplished, to attain full maturity. He also wanted to reflect upon the nature of our life together.

The question that interested Aristotle passionately had also been a passionate interest of his predecessors, especially Socrates and Plato. It is a timeless question, one of concern to anyone wishing to live his or her life to the full, and to parents wanting to point their children in the right direction, in accordance with certain values. What kind of education leads to a life that is fully human? What should be taught and how should it be taught? There are also social and political implications. Indeed, the task of any government is to organize society in such a way that the largest possible number of people can live well within it.

What is original about Aristotle and what distinguishes him from his predecessors is his desire to establish an actual moral science: the science of man. This science, he states quite clearly, does not have the same certainties as metaphysics or mathematics. It has its own certainties, however, about which we will speak later in this chapter, and it has its own methods.

We are going to discover with Aristotle, step by step, how, in his view, each one of us can orient our life in the best possible direction in order to achieve real maturity and live our humanity to the full.

The Starting Point of Aristotelian Ethics
This starting point is very simple: Every human being acts

with a view to some good. We incline towards something. We walk because doing so gives us pleasure, gets us in shape, and enables us to see interesting things. We study to achieve qualifications, which in turn will enable us to obtain employment. Pleasure, health, work are as many, good ends and reasons for our actions. Hence Aristotle's statement: "The good is that to which all things aim." Obviously, we are not talking here about good as the opposite of evil, but about a movement of attraction and tendency, in the sense of *tending towards*, that exists between a thing and its good. It is the tendency of a plant towards the sun, towards its nourishment, the tendency to growth and fullness of life through its flowering and bearing of fruit. That is its good. It is the attraction of a little girl to her mother, of man to woman, etc. This tendency, this impetus is called *desire*.

By the same token, in human affairs, all action and all sciences seek and desire their good. Health is the good that medicine seeks; victory that at which strategy aims.

> *Every art and every inquiry, and similarly every action and human pursuit, is thought to aim at some good; and for this reason the good has rightly been declared to be that to which all things aim.* (NE 1094a1–3)

This definition could cause us to go astray. Aristotle does not at the outset actually provide any indication of what constitutes the good: of what we should do or what might prevail upon our consciousness. Rather, he observes and reveals what seems to him to be its strongest characteristic: The good attracts; it is desired. It is the good that is at the origin of desire. Those looking for precise criteria for good action might well find this unsatisfactory. We are so easily mistaken about what is good! We shall see, however, how profound Aristotle's observation (or *first principle*, as philosophers call it) is and how it already gives direction to many things in his ethics.

That is not all. Not only is "the good that at which all things aim," but different "goods" form a hierarchy. We want health in order to study. We study in order to find work. If we find a job, we do so in order to have an income . . . and so on and so on. There is an ultimate motivation that is at the origin of all our actions.

> *If then, there is some end of the things we do, which we desire for its own sake (everything else being desired for the sake of this), and if we do not choose everything for the sake of something else (for at that rate the process would go on to infinity so that our desire would be empty and vain), clearly this must be the good and the chief good.* (NE 1094a18–21)

Thus Aristotle reasons,

> *Will not the knowledge of it, then, have a great influence on life? Shall we not, like archers who have a mark to aim at, be more likely to hit upon what is right?* (NE 1094a22–24)

It is so much easier to set one's sights on a target that is known. The metaphor of the archer is a pertinent one. Today, as always, many people are not interested in the target, that is to say, the ultimate end of their actions. They are prompted by *what everyone wants* — as if their family, society, and the media were determining their development.

Of course they want success, pleasure, recognition, but without really knowing why. They are caught up in short-term projects that prevent them from thinking about the purpose and meaning of human life. What do they want? They do not know. Moral science is there to help each one of us to reflect. "What do you want out of life? Who do you want to be? Don't you realize that you are responsible for your own life?"

Of course this requires a certain degree of maturity, the capacity to think, to question ourselves, and to really want to realize our full potential as human beings. As far as Aristotle is concerned, therefore, not just anyone can study moral science. That is why he does not encourage young people to engage in this field of inquiry. In fact, moral science is a practical science; it culminates in a concrete choice in life. For Aristotle, a system of ethics that remained exclusively in the realms of the abstract would not be a truly ethical approach. To undertake such study, therefore, we must have the desire to opt for the real good, the chief good. This requires maturity. The desire in itself is not enough. A certain experience of life is also necessary. And in the case of many young people, this experience is obscured by desires and passions:

> *Hence a young man is not a proper hearer of lecturers on political science* [which implies ethics]; *for he is inexperienced in the actions that occur in life, but its discussions start from these and are about these; and, further, since he tends to follow his passions, his study will be vain and unprofitable, because the end aimed at is not knowledge but action.* (NE 1095a2–5)

5

Reflections on this Starting Point

Let us therefore come back to the starting point of Aristotle's ethics, for it determines what follows. What Aristotle is propounding is not an ethics of law, or an ethics that take the form of a categorical imperative. His starting point is a fact: We human beings are drawn to ends; we desire them, we want to possess them, consume them, be one with them; we want to look at them, contemplate them, take our delight in them. That is an experience of desire. Whether it stems from our corporeal appetites or our spiritual potency, it is always an experience of attraction, an inclination, a movement that draws us consciously towards an end. In Aristotle, the subject who acts experiences ethics as the *ethics of desire*.

Desire: The term has a much wider meaning in Aristotle than in our contemporary understanding, where it is invariably tinged with passion. *Orexis*, for which — in line with many others[1] — we have used the word "desire," is a generic term that, for Aristotle, encompasses not only the passions but also the will or "rational appetite." Experience might suggest to us that the impulses of passion are not the same as those of the will. But Aristotle uses a single generic word, *orexis* or "desire," to designate that attraction which makes us rush towards what we perceive to be the good.

According to Aristotle, to adopt an ethical approach thus supposes that we set about listening to what it is that profoundly attracts us and that we familiarize ourselves with the kind of vision that sees things as moving in conformity with desire. This, far more than any sense of law, is the ethical person's prime virtue. But then we are afraid of desire and of our desires. We are afraid of going overboard, afraid of not being able to identify, among our many desires, those that are the most profound and the most true.

All the same, an ethics of desire is good news for us at a time when we have become allergic to the ethics of law. Respect for the law, simply because it is the law, will no longer do — not for young people, nor even to the same extent for the not so young. The law can no longer be imposed from outside. And even if it does impose itself on our reason as a universal law that concerns us as "rational beings," it does not necessarily have any impact on the most profound driving forces of our action. Today people want to live, to experiment with things, and, what is more, we want those things to thrill us. Here Aristotle meets some of the requirements of contemporary feeling by bringing us back to experience, by inviting us to look within ourselves at what attracts us, but also to distinguish the superficial from the more profound, to identify and shed light on what is in our inner depths. If we are to remain on course, the ethics of desire must be combined with a sense of discernment and choice, something that is clearly lacking in our culture.

Desires and Desire

As soon as we start to talk about an ethics of desire, a major objection springs to light: Following one's desires can lead people to dissipation and breakdown. We have only to look at those young people who do follow their desires and who break out and down! Isn't this really a cry for help from young people unable to identify their fundamental hearts' desire, the deepest, most unifying desire, the one that is going to help them to become fully human?

We know ourselves what it is to experience conflicting desires. We are torn in different directions. We would like to please a friend, but at the same time want to be alone to get on with our own affairs. We would like to smoke, but are afraid of destroying our lungs. We want to study, but at the same time we would like to go to the cinema. Is there, among these conflicting pulls, one supreme good that is sought after for its own sake? Is there a fundamental desire that impels us to seek other "goods" in order to achieve the conquest of that fundamental desire, the one that governs all others?

Yes, says Aristotle, what we are looking for in all our probings, the supreme good at which we are so maladroitly aiming, has a name: happiness.

> *Verbally there is very general agreement; for both the general run of men and people of superior refinement say that it is happiness and identify living well and doing well with being happy.* (NE 1095a17)

The desire for happiness is the keystone of human conduct, observes Aristotle. It is the goal above all other goals. This means that his ethics are also the ethics of happiness. As modern psychoanalysis and psychology now emphasize, a unifying principle lies at the root of our action. Every human being, including the sick or psychologically damaged person, seeks to fulfill one fundamental desire that is like the keystone to that person's behaviour. In the wounded person — and we are all wounded — this desire may have remained infantile and keep the person in a state of non-freedom, as when, for example, someone is unconsciously seeking parental approval for every choice he makes, for his choice of profession, his choice of partner. So often people live for an ideology and are incapable of recognizing their own deepest desires. The role of therapy is to help people discover the ideology that governs them so that they can choose freely and not be governed by fear and guilt.

Above and beyond these psychological impairments, and even within them, human action may be understood in terms of the desire for happiness present in our hearts. And on this unifying principle everyone is more or less agreed — on its name at least, if not on its constitution. When it comes to actually defining happiness, opinions vary.

> *But with regard to what happiness is they differ, and the many do not give the same account as the wise. For the former think it is some plain and obvious thing, like pleasure, wealth, or honour; they differ, however, from one another* — *and often even the same man identifies it with different things, with health when he is ill, with wealth when he is poor; but conscious of their ignorance, they admire those who proclaim some great ideal that is above their comprehension. Now some* [Plato and his disciples] *thought that apart from many goods there is another which is self-subsistent and causes the goodness of all these as well.* (NE 1095a20–27)

We should note, furthermore, that Aristotle has faith in nature in general, and in human nature in particular. If in every human being there is a desire for happiness, then happiness is possible. Nature is not an evil genius that makes us see some inaccessible mirage. Nature is good. It does nothing in vain. Just as the seed planted in the ground unfailingly yields flowers and then fruit, so human beings can progress to happiness — not unfailingly in their case, but provided they identify it, seek it, make good choices, and understand that its attainment may take a lifetime.

In some people, the prospect of a deliberate and conscious pursuit of happiness cannot be taken for granted: It gives rise to a sort of guilt. "Do I have the right to seek happiness when so many people are suffering and unhappy?" they ask themselves. It is a guilt that is all the more paradoxical for the fact that it can coexist quite comfortably, in the contemporary mind, with the pursuit of pleasure. Here again, Aristotle helps us to take stock of what it is we really want. It would be strange if a man were to refuse to exercise his calling as a man, a calling upon which his life depended and which is his most precious good, at the whim of his impulses.

What Do We Conceive Happiness to Be?

What do people say about happiness? Where do they look for it? In pleasure, wealth, honours: No area, Aristotle intimates, can be ruled out. The pursuit of possessions and pleasure is almost second nature in our consumer culture, and just as many people as ever scramble about in pursuit of honours, so eager are we for recognition. So what do the wise have to tell us? Should we give up all these material things and project our desire onto a higher plane? Given all the forms of spiritual wisdom centred on interiority, there has been no shortage of people throughout history to defend the suppression of desires as a condition of happiness. Today, however, Plato and the Stoics in particular seem to produce fewer rivals to Aristotle than certain Eastern mystics. Union with the good within is less attractive than the promise of suppression of stress through inner emptiness.

But it is not Aristotle's style to ignore the realities of this world and progress too quickly to the things of the spirit. He examines the opinion of the general run of people, who do not separate aspirations to happiness from pleasure, honours, and wealth. What he found in his day is still valid today.

Consider pleasure: You don't have to be an unbridled sensualist to recognize the kind of happiness and life associated with pleasure. It is a view found just as readily in the man who goes to work, builds his house, or takes care of his family. He thinks that there are things that bring work and hardship and things that bring happiness, the pleasures of life that we might experience on holiday or in retirement: travel, congenial company, good food, the latest fashions. In short, having a good time. But when we think about it properly . . .

> *It would, indeed, be strange if the end were amusement, and one were to take trouble and suffer hardship all one's life in order to amuse oneself. . . . Now to exert oneself and work for the sake of amusement seems silly and utterly childish. But to amuse oneself in order that one may exert oneself . . . seems right; for amusement is a sort of relaxation, and we need relaxation because we cannot work continuously. Relaxation, then, is not an end; for it is taken for the sake of activity.*
>
> *The happy life is thought to be virtuous;[2] now a virtuous life requires exertion, and does not consist in amusement. And we say that serious things are better*

than laughable things and those connected with amusement, and that the activity of the better of any two things . . . is the more serious; but the activity of the better is ipso facto superior and more of the nature of happiness. (NE 1176b28–1177a7)

Another axis of the quest for happiness is honours. The pursuit of honours is primarily a characteristic of cultivated people.

People of superior refinement and of active disposition identify happiness with honour; for this is roughly speaking, the end of the political life. (NE 1095b22)

With politicians we may include powerful people in general, all those in authority in the economic, financial, or religious domain. The pursuit of honours can also affect men of science. It is as if the higher our standing is, the more we are tempted by visible signs of recognition. The more noble our achievements, the more we are tempted by others' admiration. In ancient Greek times, a statue in our honour; nowadays, a street, a library, a public building named after us, or some other such distinction. So much for visible signs; other people may be more interested in fame or success. All their energy is directed at winning a place in the hearts of those around them or of their "public," at being admired, at cultivating an image.

But it seems too superficial to be what we are looking for, since it is thought to depend on those who bestow honour rather than on him who receives it, but the good we divine to be something proper to a man and not easily taken from him. (NE 1095b24–26)

There precisely is the limitation of honour: It depends on others for its existence. Doesn't happiness depend more upon ourselves?

As for the accumulation of wealth, profit for profit's sake, it removes us even further from the idea we have of happiness, for riches are for the sake of other things: power, esteem, pleasure, friends. They do not have the value of a *final end.* Would the removal of these "goods" be enough to strip us of our happiness? Isn't happiness something deeper?

> *The life of money-making is one undertaken under compulsion, and wealth is evidently not the good we are seeking; for it is merely useful and for the sake of something else.* (NE 1096a6)

The good, or happiness, is to be sought in another direction. We must trust our intuition: happiness is something deeper within us, something that cannot be wrested from us like some object, and it is also a reality that is sufficient in itself because it is the highest end of our desires — the ultimate and perfect end, the one at which all our activity is directed.

> *Now we call that which is in itself worthy of pursuit more final than that which is worthy of pursuit for the sake of something else, and that which is never desirable for the sake of something else more final than the things that are desirable both in themselves and for the sake of that other thing. . . . Now such a thing happiness,*

above all else, is held to be; for this we choose always for itself and never for the sake of something else, but honour, pleasure, reason, and every virtue we choose indeed for themselves (for if nothing resulted from them we should still choose each of them), but we choose them also for the sake of happiness, judging that by means of them we shall be happy. Happiness, on the other hand, no one chooses for the sake of these, nor, in general, for anything other than itself. (NE 1097a30–b7)

This leads Aristotle to state that happiness is self-sufficient, which is to say that it is not sought after for the sake of anything else.

The self-sufficient we now define as that which when isolated makes life desirable and lacking in nothing; and such we think happiness to be. (NE 1097b14–16)

What Is this Supreme Good?
We need to understand a little better what happiness is, of what it consists.

A clearer account of what it is is still desired. This might perhaps be given, if we could first ascertain the function of man. For just as for a flute-player, a sculptor, or any artist, and, in general, for all things that have a function or activity, the good and the "well" is thought to reside in the function, so would it seem to be for man, if he has a function. (NE 1097b21–27)

Does man have a function or activity of his own? Of that there is no doubt.

*Have the carpenter, then, and the tanner certain func-
tions or activities, and has man none? Is he born without
a function? Or as eye, hand, foot, and in general each of
the parts evidently has a function, may one lay it down
that man similarly has a function apart from all these?
What then can this be?* (NE 1097b28–33)

This brings us to the definition of happiness according
to Aristotle.

The activity or function distinctive to man should be
sought in connection with what is peculiar to him, in what
defines him most particularly. Aristotle, in common with
all the other ancient Greeks, saw man as a being endowed
with reason (*logos*). His activity is either "obedience to reason" or the "exercise of thought." Thus man's good is an
"activity of the soul in accordance with reason." And this
activity must be well performed and excellent, that is to
say, "an activity of the soul in accordance with virtue, and
if there are more than one virtue, in accordance with the
best and the most complete." (NE 1098a7–17)

What Are We to Make of this Definition?

The entire ethics of happiness is governed by three words:
logos, virtue, and *activity.* Happiness, maintains Aristotle, is
an activity in accordance with the *logos.* If we interpret *logos*
as "reason" or "rule," it makes his ethics very rational! We
must therefore deepen the meaning of the word. In the
Greek culture of his day, it was a word laden with significance
that cannot be conveyed in a single English word. "Of all the
words in the *Ethics, logos* is the most difficult to translate,"
writes W. D. Ross in his excellent translation of the *Ethics.*[3]

The Logos

For Aristotle, what defines the human being — what distinguishes him from the animals — is reason, the *logos*. Man is a rational animal, capable of reflecting and thinking. Perhaps in our day the difference between animals and human beings has been somewhat obscured. We talk about dolphins' intelligence and their capacity to communicate with one another; we talk about the community life of bees, about the intelligence and goodness of cats and dogs. There is certainly affection and communication between some animals, but man, alone among animals, seeks, progresses, evolves, is in a state of constant movement towards something else. For centuries, cows have lived in their fields, grazing on grass. Their eyes lack depth; in them there is little anguish. Human beings, by contrast, are deeply anguished. They are constantly looking for the keys to happiness.

Erasmus said in *The Praise of Folie* that human beings were the most calamitous of animals because while all the others were reconciled to living within the limits of their nature, humans alone tried to exceed those limits. Is that not the drama of man in search of the infinite, of the "ever more" — of more power, more wealth, more love and freedom, more understanding of life and God? Is it not this thirst for the infinite that drives humanity, generation after generation, to go further, to make new discoveries, to evolve towards the new, in a way that (so man believes) will enable him to transcend suffering and death?

In order to appreciate this distinction peculiar to man,

we cannot confine ourselves to the Darwinian view, which is restricted to the biological. We must contemplate man from the point of view of his fruits, his actions, and his works. All human undertakings bear the stamp of a desire for the infinite, right down to the desire for infinite enjoyment or infinite power. This is proof that there is something special about man that makes him man. Aristotle called this difference *logos*.

For the ancient Greeks *logos* also meant the theory, science, or definition of a reality and even the written or spoken word that denoted it. But if *logos* means definition, it is because things are knowable. So it is that we can say, by extending Aristotle's thinking and explicitly expressing the truths contained in what he says, that *logos* is intimately related to the light in every human being that enables him to be known; it grasps the *intelligibility* or meaning of every being. This *logos* is not just formal definition. At a more profound level it is the reflection of the light in everything that stems not only from what that thing is, but also from its origins and the end towards which it tends. That is why Aristotle tells us in his works that "the final cause is *logos* and *logos* is the starting point" (De Part. 639b15), for it is from the vantage point of the final cause — the reason for which a thing is done — that the thing can be properly understood. To understand the *logos* of a leaf, for example, we need to know what it is, what it is made of, how it emerges from the branch, how it is nourished by the earth and the roots, how it takes in the sun's rays and emits gases into the universe. We need to know how all the leaves on the trees have an effect on the climate of a place, and how finally each leaf falls, feeds the earth after having been nourished by it and enables animals and human beings to live. The leaf is bound up with the movement of life towards death, and of death towards life. The *logos* of the leaf, and therefore of everything, is much more than a rational definition. It is the leaf in its relationship with the tree, the earth, the sun, the climate, and other living things. *Logos* implies and seeks a true vision of the world.

But *logos* is also that which enables us to grasp that light in other things, to know them, to understand them, to comprehend the different causes of their being. It is the intelligence insofar as it is the light capable of grasping what is luminous in things, the intelligence that seeks intimate contact with reality. *Logos* is close to the mind without being coldly and purely intellectual. At its behest, our whole being, including our sensual and affective powers, launches itself towards the real, confident that this effort will not be in vain. This movement that carries us outwards is very different from a knowledge that proceeds from interiority, as argued by Plato, who was convinced that the good must be sought within oneself. It is very different from the effort directed at consciousness of self.

Logos is simultaneously the intelligence (*nous* in Greek) that grasps principles intuitively and the discursive intelligence, which reasons on the basis of principles. Thus *logos* is a light that enables us to contemplate, understand, reason, order, name, control, and regulate. *Logos* is no longer therefore merely the discursive intelligence that we call reason; it is the principle within us that enables us to understand and govern ourselves. It manifests itself as a light, which is also a rule. If we refer to the text in which Aristotle says that *logos* is the final, that is to say, the principal cause, the cause that gives a thing its ultimate significance, we can also say that *logos* is the light that enables us to realize our full potential, to attain our end, be it through the exercise of the noblest activity or through an activity in accordance with the light, which then becomes the rule or the law that leads to that end.

Thus the definition of man as "a being having *logos*" could be more faithfully expressed as "a being possessing an inner light capable of grasping the light in others, of thereby becoming autonomous and steering itself towards the light." *Light* here should not be taken in its mystical sense, but in the sense of that which is luminous to the mind, in the same way that we might say something has had light shed upon it when our minds have understood it.

And the definition of happiness as "activity in accordance with *logos*" becomes that activity in man which is the finest, the greatest, and springs from the light that is in him. But how can all this be conveyed in a few words? That is the difficulty of any translation.

Virtue

In order to understand happiness better as "an activity stemming from *logos* in accordance with virtue," we must also understand the word *virtue*, which recurs constantly in Aristotelian ethics. In contemporary culture the word has a negative resonance. Isn't there something slightly rigid about virtuous people? Aren't they inclined to be restricted by laws, and not much fun?

Virtue, according to Aristotle, is a human being's capacity to act well, think well, or produce a good work. It implies excellence. To be a good zither player, you need musical aptitude, you have to learn to play the zither, and you have to practise. It is only at the point when you can play the zither competently and with ease and joy, that you have the virtue of being a zither player. Before you acquire this virtue you may perhaps be able to play, but not with the degree of facility that makes it second nature to you. For Aristotle the intellectual virtues come first: the principles of art, science, prudence, wisdom, and intelligence. It is a question of developing these intellectual capacities, of achieving excellence in this domain so that we may possess intellectual virtues. But that is not all. In order to be truly human and lead a fully human life, we need a certain substance or inner structure to enable us to act correctly, respect others' rights, be our own masters, speak the truth, and be upright and honest.

> *For no man would maintain that he is happy who has not in him a particle of courage or temperance or justice or prudence, who is afraid of every insect that flutters past him, and will commit any crime, however great, in order to gratify his lust for meat or drink, who will sacrifice his dearest friend for the sake of half-a-farthing, and is as feeble and false in mind as a child or a madman.* (Pol. 1323a27–33)

This inner structure, which saves us from total disintegration, is moral virtue, and it too is considered to be an excellence. A man may perform a courageous act without possessing the entire virtue of courage. Virtue is an excellence that enables him to act courageously with a certain facility and joy. He is somehow drawn to courage. Happiness then, "activity stemming from *logos* in accordance with virtue," implies that the person has acquired a certain knowledge, has practised it, and can now act humanly, with a degree of excellence, facility, and joy. This is the domain of human virtue, or ethics.

Happiness as an Activity

In Aristotle's definition, happiness is not therefore a state, but a vital activity proceeding from within each human being. Happiness, for Aristotle, is not the lot of someone who peacefully and comfortably enjoys his possessions, who is content with his family, work, success, riches, and honours, or is satisfied with himself. Happiness is a vital activity that brings immense joy and that is life. It is the completely joyous activity of one who is entirely, with his intelligence and his whole being, oriented towards that which is nobler and greater than himself. This life that is an activity, however, implies that we first work on our selves. It involves study and discipline.

We should remember here that, for Aristotle, there are two forms of activity: one that aims at the creation of an object outside oneself (the production of a book, the manufacture of a thing, the creation of a piece of artwork) and the other, which is not aimed at anything external — it is an immanent activity. The joy of this activity derives not from what it produces but from the activity itself. So it is that some artists will speak of the ecstatic joy they experience when they are writing poetry or painting a picture. When the work is finished, sometimes they are disappointed. This artistic activity is not an entirely immanent act because an object is produced in the process, but it comes close to it. For Aristotle the most perfectly immanent activity is the pursuit of contemplation, the vision of truth. We shall look at that, in Chapter 3.

Happiness as a vital activity touches on important moral questions for today. Is human life merely a matter of being successful, of doing one's work and performing one's civic and familial duties well? Is human happiness *resting* in the awareness that we have lived successfully, have been awarded honours, and are surrounded by our family and friends? Where, in that case, do celebration and passion belong? Isn't happiness for some people today more readily associated with exciting activities and moments of exaltation and enthusiasm? Everyday life can appear so dreary, repetitive, and boring. And when life does not provide us with exciting moments, we sometimes try to find them in a frenzy of eating, drinking, alcohol, or drugs, for example. Of course we must work, of course there must be order and we must do our duty, but isn't happiness to be found rather in some pleasurable activity?

Aristotle's view is that we should aim higher. We should find that vital activity that proceeds from the deepest part of ourselves and brings with it immense joy. This joy derives not only from the work accomplished but from the activity itself, stemming from deep within us. Happiness lies not in the capacity to act but in the experience of life lived to the full, which brings tremendous joy. We shall speak of this later in this chapter, in connection with the nature of pleasure and joy in Aristotle.

Joy of Living

Aristotle's genius consists of having recognized the joy of living associated with our consciousness of activity. The following passage on friendship indicates that this immense joy is not simply that of attaining the object of our desires, but the joy of feeling alive and of existing through an activity.

> But if life itself is good and pleasant (which it seems to be, from the very fact that all men desire it, and particularly those who are good and supremely happy; for to such men life is most desirable, and their existence is the most supremely happy); and if he who sees perceives that he sees, and he who hears, that he hears, and he who walks, that he walks, and in the case of all other activities similarly there is something which perceives that we are active, so that if we perceive, we perceive that we perceive, and if we think, that we think; and if to perceive that we perceive or think is to perceive that we exist (for existence was defined as perceiving or thinking); and if perceiving that one lives is in itself one of the things that are pleasant (for life is by nature good, and to perceive what is good present in oneself is pleasant); and if life is desirable, and particularly so for good men, because to them existence is good and pleasant (for they are pleased at the consciousness of the presence in them of what is in itself good); and if as the virtuous man is to himself, he is to his friend also (for his friend is another self): — if all this be true, as his own being is desirable for each man, so, or almost so, is that of his friend . . . (NE 1170a24–b5)

The consciousness of self referred to here is not the consciousness of having lived a good life, it is an *experience of life*. As we shall see, this vital activity always has an object at which it aims, an object that is looked at, loved, contemplated. It is not just consciousness of our self, of our life and existence, but consciousness of our self being oriented towards another or towards the truth contemplated. It is as if there is a twofold joy: the joy of the presence of the object seen and contemplated, but also the joy of feeling that we live and exist in and through this union with the object that is sought after and loved. We are a long way from the consciousness of self sought by some modern philosophies or the consciousness of the self through emptiness found in some forms of Eastern mysticism. There is perhaps a form of consciousness of self to be found in emptiness, but that is not Aristotle's vision. For him, consciousness of self stems from the presence of the desired object.

In order to realize his full potential, to be fully alive and conscious of living and existing, man needs an object outside himself. This is because man is not perfect in himself. He is an integral part of the world. He is not the *whole* of the universe. He is not God. He did not ask to be born and has great difficulty in confronting the fact that he must die and disappear. He has received his existence, his body, his intelligence, and it is through his body and his senses that he relates to the universe and to others, for all knowledge, for Aristotle, comes initially from the senses. Man is situated in a reality of which he has a vital need. He has not created what is real; he is called to know it, to understand, see, and contemplate it. He can also modify it, have an effect upon it, but only within certain limits that respect that reality.

Aristotle's ethics are set within his vision of the world. Because man is a body, he is subject to changes, fatigue, illness, death, to the thousand requirements necessary for his body and soul to function well. Happiness is thus not to be divorced from the body; it implies an integration of the body and its frailties. That is where Aristotle parts company with his master and friend, Plato, for whom the soul seeks to separate itself from the body in order to rejoin the idea of the good. Aristotle is a realist.

> *How, then, is it that no one is continuously pleased? Is it that we grow weary? Certainly all human things are incapable of continuous activity.* (NE 1175a3–4)

Yet happiness itself demands continuous activity, because it is nowhere other than in activity. And for this reason, among others, contemplative activity constitutes happiness. Paradoxically, it is the least tiring of all our activities.

> *It is the most continuous, since we can contemplate truth more continuously than we can do anything.* (NE 1177a22–23)

Bios *and* Zoe

In "vital activity" there is *life*. What we actually do, however, is not always an expression of life. It does not always exude great vitality. Our life is not always pitched at a truly vibrant level. How then can this desire for immense happiness be reconciled with everyday life and all its many functions, with our family and social life, our education and work? Aristotle's genius lies in his association of the supreme and vital activity with one's lifetime as a whole.

In Greek there are two words for life: *bios* and *zoe*. *Bios* means life as a whole, the different states or different forms of life. (*Bios* does not in any way refer to animal life, as the word "biology" might lead us to expect. That etymological connection would be misleading here.) Hence the way Aristotle uses it when he refers to happiness being the best activity "in a complete life [*bios*]" (NE 1098a18). He uses the same term when he speaks of the political life (*bios politicos*) or the contemplative life (*bios theoretikos*), but in the case of vital activity, he uses *zoe*. *Zoe* is that which gives life, renders us alive, makes us want to live, grow, and be. "Life [*zoe*] seems to be common even to plants" (NE 1097b33).

It can happen that our whole life is taken up with vital activity. Once a man has discovered and tested out the fact that happiness lies in a perfect activity aimed at realizing or contemplating the most perfect object possible, he may direct his whole life (*bios*) towards this blissful and vital activity (*zoe*). He orients his life in such a way as to accomplish himself perfectly either through a purely intellectual activity or through a political role, in helping his fellow citizens to attain happiness. He will also have his family life, his work in society, and his friends, and all these will be oriented towards certain moments of blissful activity.

That does not mean to say that he will not enjoy good food, his job in society, his family life, or his friends. Aristotle does not overlook the fact that these intermediary goods are desirable and bring joy and real brightness. They are real and important human values, but in the final analysis they are oriented towards the principal excellent activity.

The distinction between *bios* and *zoe* is not unrelated to that which exists between an intermediary end and the ultimate end.

> *To us it is clear from what has been said that happiness is among the things that are prized and perfect. It seems to be so also from the fact that it is a first principle; for it is for the sake of this that we do all that we do, and the first principle and cause of goods is, we claim, something prized and divine.* (NE 1102a1–4)

Someone told me recently about a head of personnel in a large American company who wanted to make all those dependent on him as happy as possible. He sent each one a questionnaire asking, among other things, what activity in life interested them most, what made them feel most alive, gave them the most joy, and held the most value for them. He then helped his staff to realize that all their other activities took on meaning as a result of that principal activity, and to organize their lives accordingly. Once we appreciate that some tedious activities can help us to know a finer activity that will give meaning to our entire life, they become less irksome. Without realizing it, this man had been using Aristotle's methods!

If happiness is to be found in some marvellous activity, it is also the fruit of an entire life. It is the

> *. . . activity of soul in accordance with virtue, in accordance with the best and most complete. But we must add in "a complete life." For one swallow does not make a summer, nor does one day; and so too one day, or a short time, does not make a man blessed and happy.* (NE 1098a18–20)

This enables us to extend our horizon. If life is a long-term accomplishment, man has time in which to learn. This is something to reassure contemporary man, obsessed as he is with action. Moral evaluation can only be complete if it takes into account an entire lifetime.

Thus it is not a matter of happily shutting ourselves away in splendid isolation. It is a matter of working with and for others. When it is said that happiness is self-sufficient,

> ... *we do not mean that which is sufficient for a man by himself, for one who lives a solitary life, but also for parents, children, wife, and in general for his friends and fellow citizens, since man is born for citizenship.* (NE 1097b7–10)

Aristotle notes, moreover, that we ought not to live (*bios*) at all costs. Our life time is to be lived (*zoe*) and lived intensely "but some acts, perhaps, we cannot be forced to do, but ought rather to face death after the most fearful sufferings" (NE 1110a27). Was he thinking of Socrates, who accepted death rather than submit to an iniquitous judgement that went against his conscience?

> [The good man] *will face great dangers, and when he is in danger he is unsparing of his life, knowing that there are conditions on which life is not worth having.* (NE 1124b8)

> *It is true of the good man too that he does many acts for the sake of his friends and his country, and if necessary dies for them; for he will throw away both wealth and honours and in general the goods that are objects of*

*competition, gaining for himself nobility; since he would
prefer a short period of intense pleasure to a long one of
mild enjoyment, a twelve-month of noble life to many
years of humdrum existence, and one great and noble
action to many trivial ones. Now those who die for others doubtless attain this result.* (NE 1169a18–25)

Is Happiness a Gift of God?

Happiness appears to have a fragile quality to it. We can
work at it, but some things, such as good or bad fortune,
seem not to depend entirely on us. It is not just a question
of being lucky when it comes to money or goods. It is a
fact that people are not born equal. We have different
capacities, dispositions, and gifts; our health varies from
one individual to the next; we have different families and
education. These are all factors that appear to condition
our happiness. How can I develop as fully as possible if I
have not had the necessary education?

*For this reason also the question is asked, whether hap-
piness is to be acquired by learning or by habituation or
some other sort of training, or come in virtue of some divine
providence or again by chance. Now if there is any gift of
the gods to men, it is reasonable that happiness should be
god-given, and most surely god-given of all human things
inasmuch as it is the best.* (NE 1099b10–14)

Aristotle admits that the gods may be directly responsible for our good fortune, which would also make it
securely based, but he refuses to identify happiness purely
and simply with good fortune.

For clearly if we were to keep pace with his fortunes, we should often call the same man happy and again wretched, making the happy man out to be a "chameleon and insecurely based." Or is this keeping pace with his fortunes quite wrong? Success or failure in life does not depend on these, but human life, as we said, needs these as mere additions, while virtuous activities or their opposites are what constitute happiness or the reverse. (NE 1100b4–10)

Marie-Dominique Philippe writes in his *Introduction to the Philosophy of Aristotle* of how happiness is in part acquired, in part derived from divine favour, and in part the work of chance, and of how virtuous activity is the fruit of human labour, while the goods of nature and external goods seem to depend upon divine favour and chance.

The word for happiness in Greek, *eudaimonia*, is hard to translate. It is difficult to take a word so laden with meaning and translate it by using an English word that has been subject to all the fluctuations of culture. The root of the word *eudaimonia* is actually *daimon*, which originally meant "the god who dispenses goods." It was a natural progression from "the one who distributes the portions" to the portions themselves. The *eudaimon* is thus the one who has received a "good share" dispensed by the divinity. The "good share" may refer, as in Heraclitus, for example, to character rather than to favourable events, or to the possession of material goods.

It is his own character that is each man's daimon. (Heraclitus, Fr. 119)

> *Of the kind of soul that is the principle in us, we should note that it is God who gives it to each one of us as a* daimon. (Plato, "Timaeus," 90A)

Aristotle makes little use of the word *daimon*, but does take from his predecessors the idea of this element of fortune being indispensable to happiness: indispensable, but not sufficient in itself. It is not enough to rely alone on a well-born character, talents, or a fortunate circumstance. It is for each man to work his soul towards virtue, that is to say, to achieve the fullest possible development as a human being at the level of his character or his intelligence. If the word *eudaimonia* originally had passive connotations, in that we receive a good or bad share, it has gradually assumed the meaning of a certain activity: Whether we are good or bad is our own responsibility.

To understand Aristotle we have to bear in mind the precise meaning with which he imbues the words "happiness" and "unhappiness." Happiness is perfect activity, unhappiness arises from bad activity. And in order to experience happy and fulfilling activity, we must have made clear choices in order to orient our life in a specific direction: that of becoming fully human.

Conclusion: The Principles and Method of the Ethics
Aristotle's definition of happiness is clear: it is an activity of *logos*, or at least one which involves exercising *logos*, that activity being made perfect by virtue. All his ethics derive from this truth. But how does Aristotle arrive at this truth?

In order to work out his system of morals, Aristotle

relied upon the opinion of wise men and of the general assembly of men. In order to know what is good for man, let us ask men; let's not look at theories and ideologies, but rather at facts. Let us listen to men, especially to those considered to be the wisest and most human.

> *For we say that that which every one thinks really is so: and the man who attacks this belief will hardly have anything more credible to maintain instead.* (NE 1172b39–1173a4)

> *For no one in his senses would make a proposition of what no one holds, nor yet make a problem of what is obvious to everybody or to most people: for the latter admits of no doubt, while to the former no one would assent.* (Top. 104a7)

> *These opinions are "generally accepted" which are accepted by every one or by the majority, or by the most notable or illustrious of them.* (Top.100b21–23)

> *We believe good men more fully and more readily than others: this is true generally whatever the question is, and absolutely true where exact certainty is impossible and opinions are divided.* (Rhet. 1356a5–8)

That is why on every page of the *Ethics* we find the word *doxa*, which may be translated as "in everyone's opinion" or "according to general opinion." But be careful! Opinion, like the likely or the probable, is not, in Aristotle, as with some of his predecessors, synonymous with what is false. Unlike Socrates, who placed those who lived by opinion "which does not know the truth" in opposition to those "who know," Aristotle makes room for opinion in knowledge.

Obviously, however, there's opinion and then there's opinion. When Aristotle talks of generally accepted opinion, he is not referring to opinion polls or the results of propaganda. He knows that most men follow their passions and, as we would recognize today, have difficulty in resisting the pressure to conform. In common sense, Aristotle is looking for something deeper that is nevertheless shared by all: good sense, the opinion of the ordinary man whose judgement is based on a natural sense of right and wrong and not influenced by his passions or by propaganda pressure. This kind of general opinion can be a path to wisdom, especially on the subject of human beings. How can we rediscover the faith that Aristotle had in general opinion? How can we identify the real sages of our time? Who are the people capable of sound judgement?

Not only does Aristotle make room for opinion in his moral science, but he is also prepared to be satisfied with the probable. This is another characteristic of the method used in his *Ethics*: He does not expect to apply the same standards of precision as in arithmetic.

> *These, then, are the ends at which our inquiry aims* [what is good for man and for the city], *since it is political science, in one sense of that term. Our discussion will be adequate if it has as much clearness as the subject-matter admits of, for precision is not to be sought for alike in all discussions, any more than in all the products of crafts.* (NE 1094b10–14)

We must be content, then, in speaking of such subjects
[ethics] *and with such premises to indicate the truth
roughly and in outline, and in speaking about such
things which are for the most part true and with premises of the same kind to reach conclusions that are no
better. In the same spirit, therefore, should each type of
statement be received; for it is the mark of an educated
man to look for precision in each class of things just so far
as the nature of the subject admits; it is evidently equally
foolish to accept probable reasoning from a mathemati-
cian and to demand from a rhetorician scientific proofs.*
(NE 1094b19–28)

Why did he adopt this particular method based on
opinion and what was probable? Because the science of
ethics is a practical one, the aim of which is action in particular, concrete situations. It aims at the contingent.
Should we act in this way or that in the present situation?
This requires discernment. Opinion or what is probable
does not engender doubt but a conviction that will form
the basis of a deliberate choice. This conviction is rooted
in what, today, we call *conscience.* Certainly this conscience
must be conditioned by the opinion of wise men and by
ethics. Only then will it be a sound conviction.

Even if general opinion or that of wise men is important,
however, it must still always be tested against facts.

*The opinions of the wise seem, then, to harmonize with
our arguments. But while even such things carry some
conviction, the truth in practical matters is discerned from
the facts of life; for these are the decisive factor. We must*

therefore survey what we have already said, bringing it to the test of the facts of life, and if it harmonizes with the facts we must accept it, but if it clashes with them we must suppose it to be mere theory. (NE 1179a17–22)

As Jacques Maritain,[4] who knew Aristotle's philosophy well, tells us,

"Men's experience plays a fundamental role in his ethics. He resorts to it constantly. The conduct of prudent men, the opinion of old men and their experience of life, society's customs, are indispensable sources for him and for the very edification of moral philosophy. But he makes use of all this human experience to bring out by induction the rational principles with which it is pregnant. Hence the considerable place he affords empirical information and the abundant and involved psychological descriptions found in many chapters of the Nichomachean Ethics *and the* Eudemian Ethics.*"*

Aristotle thus presents us with a profoundly human system of morals. Knowing and living by these morals was not for him primarily a question of creating a new science of ethics, of being intellectually brilliant, but of being prepared to learn humbly from humanity, to question the men of his day and of previous days: the wisest men, those who were the most fully developed as human beings.

CHAPTER 2

PLEASURE AND FRIENDSHIP THE SPICE OF LIFE

Let us continue our journey with Aristotle and our exploration of his understanding of the fullness of human life and the means of attaining it. Aristotle is far from legalistic; all his moral thinking is centred on man and his desire for the good, a desire that permeates all human potency, from the most carnal to the most spiritual. The flesh desires its good, just as the spirit does. It is not a case of playing one potency against another, but of combining them in the interests of the happiness of the whole person, under the guidance of *logos*.

For intelligence, reason (*logos*) is not there to tyrannize us but to enlighten us, to shed light on the good, and so to draw us more effectively towards it. To put it another way, Aristotle's ethics are not coldly rational; they are human. There are two indications of this fact: the way in which Aristotle talks about pleasure and what he has to say about friendship.

Pleasure

In his ethics, Aristotle is not sparing in his treatment of pleasure, whether that of the body or that of affectivity. Leaning from the outset on general opinion that "links pleasure closely with happiness" (NE 1153b15), he affords pleasure a proper place in the pursuit of happiness. Later in this chapter we will see how pleasure is given its full and proper place, but no more than that.

Happiness is not to be divorced from pleasure:

> *Most people say that happiness involves pleasure; this is why the blessed man is called by a name derived from a word meaning enjoyment.* (NE 1152b8)

This link between the terms *makarios* (blessed) and *kairein* (to enjoy oneself) is not, it seems, very convincing to expert Hellenists. Aristotle, however, is seeking once more to show that general opinion is the indicator of something true: Happiness and pleasure go together. What, after all, would happiness be if it had no reverberation in us? Do not the gods themselves experience pleasure as the subjective dimension of their blessed state?

So bound together are happiness and pleasure that actions undertaken without pleasure do not have their full value. They are not *complete*, Aristotle tells us. They have not achieved fullness of life.

> *Every activity is completed by the attendant pleasure.* (NE 1175a20)

> *For every one it* [pleasure] *completes life.* (NE 1175a17)

It is clear then that without enjoyment there is no moral plenitude! Far from detracting from the moral or human depth of our activities, pleasure augments it. Aristotle is a balanced man, and so the desire for purity, characteristic of ethics influenced by puritanism, for example, does not cross his mind. "There is nothing human about insensitivity," he says in his chapter on temperance, a remark that might seem self-evident in any other context. In the context of a system of ethics aimed at being wholly human, it means that lack of feeling is neither virtuous nor fully moral.

The man who does not rejoice in noble actions is not even good; since no one would call a man just who did not enjoy acting justly. (NE 1099a17)

Here Aristotle is underlining a profoundly human truth that today's psychiatry and psychology would endorse: Very little of our behaviour is separable from the pursuit of pleasure — even the quest for moral purity. The satisfaction of being virtuous, of finally mastering oneself, or, less subtly, of being better than others, is a form of pleasure. This is a law of the human psyche. Aristotle, in his own day and in his own terms, recognized that fact, and was not afraid to integrate pleasure into an ethical approach.

If pleasure does not stain morality, neither does it attach itself to happiness like some artificial adornment. It is not sprinkled over a moral act to guarantee it a certain spice. Happiness and pleasure are intrinsically linked. Pleasure has a direct effect on the quality of the activity — of the vital activity that is at the heart of happiness.

Their [the lovers of what is noble] *life, therefore, has no further need of pleasure as a sort of adventitious charm, but has its pleasure in itself.* (NE 1099a15)

At this stage, Aristotle might be taken quite simply for a hedonist who identifies happiness with the experience of enjoyment. But, of course, he is not. His thinking is more refined than that. Aristotle does not in any way confuse a happy life with a life of pleasure.

What is pleasure?
We should, then, better define the nature of pleasure in relation to happiness. What *is* pleasure? The question is posed in Book X of the *Nichomachean Ethics,* in one of the most original passages propounded by Aristotle. Here we touch upon the very heart of philosophical thinking.

What is pleasant is the activity of the present, the hope of the future, the memory of the past; but what is most pleasant is that which depends on activity. (NE 1168a13)

So what is the status of pleasure in relation to activity? A sentence already quoted tells us that "pleasure completes the activities" (NE 1175a17), it crowns them and renders them more perfect.

To understand the meaning of this sentence, let us make quite sure that we appreciate what Aristotle means by *activity,* and to do that let us refer to some of the ideas behind his philosophy of knowledge. Let us take the example of knowledge pertaining to the senses: sensation.

Sensation, the activity of the senses, is ranged round two poles. At the one pole is the subject perceiving through his senses (sight, hearing, touch, taste, smell), all of which are open to objects that are sensible, in an attitude of expectation and desire. At the other pole is the object: colour, sound, heat, cold, smells, the sweet and the salty. Sensation is the "shared action of what can be sensed and the one who senses." Neither that which is sensible (the object) alone, nor the one sensing (the subject) alone, can create sensation. The subject by itself remains lifeless. The object by itself remains insensible. Bringing one into the presence of the other, however, enables the object to awaken the subject, to actualize it and produce sensation. That is, Aristotle stipulates, all being well!

If we are feeling morose or tired, and especially if our listening organ is deficient, we may well listen to music we love without enjoying it at all. In such circumstances our capacity to receive is diminished. Or, indeed, if on the other hand the musicians are bad and grate on our ears, the deficiency lies with the object. The sensation exists, but without being experienced to the full.

Activity is perfect, and therefore pleasant, when the two protagonists are both in their best possible form — when my hearing, my intelligence, and my sight have not yet faded, and when the object is as good as it can be: A poor philosopher will inspire less enthusiasm in me than a Socrates, and an established contralto more than a beginner. To put it differently, in such circumstances neither the subject nor the object presents any obstacle to the completeness of the action. That is why Aristotle speaks both of an activity that is *unimpeded* (in an earlier formulation of his thinking on pleasure) and of an activity that is *perfect* (in a more developed formulation).

The experience of discovery gives us some idea of this happy encounter between object and subject. A new object always seems more fascinating for us to discover because our sensibility is not yet tired of it. On both sides things are in a state of freshness that makes the meeting intense. Pleasure is at its peak.

> *Since every sense is active in relation to its object, and a sense which is in good condition acts perfectly in relation to the most beautiful of its objects (for perfect activity seems to be ideally of this nature; whether we say that it is active, or the organ in which it resides, may be assumed to be immaterial), it follows that in the case of each sense the best activity is that of the best-conditioned organ in relation to the finest of its objects.* (NE 1174b14–23)

"The finest activity is that which is the most pleasant." That is to say that pleasure is born of, or springs from, perfection of the activity. It is its total fulfillment and blossoming. There is no need to add any supplementary spice to the activity. It is sufficient in itself, such as when we are at a film and feel no need to eat popcorn.

> *This is why when we enjoy anything very much we do not throw ourselves into anything else, and do one thing only when we are not much pleased by another: e.g. in the theatre the people who eat sweets do so most when the actors are poor.* (NE 1175b10–14)

For every activity, then, there is a corresponding maximum pleasure that is linked to the perfection of the act. This does not prevent Aristotle from ranging pleasures in a hierarchy determined by the object pursued. The nobler the object is, the greater the pleasure. Ensuring that justice is done, for example, gives rise to greater pleasure and joy than savouring one of life's comforts. It is the object that defines the act and consequently the nobility of the pleasure.

For this reason Aristotle distinguishes between the various sources of pleasure:

> *Now of the things that produce pleasure some are necessary, while others are worthy of choice in themselves but admit of excess, the bodily causes of pleasure being necessary (by such I mean both those concerned with food and those concerned with sexual intercourse) . . . while the others are not necessary but worthy of choice in themselves (e.g. victory, honour, wealth, and good and pleasant things of this sort).* (EN 1147b24–30)

Of course, as we shall see in Chapter 5, not all pleasures are morally good. We can desire food, wine, and sexual relations to excess, just as we can desire wealth and honours to excess (NE 1154a13–18).

We can see, then, to what extent Aristotle's ethics are not just a moral system of *desire*, but also one into which *pleasure* is integrated. Desire and pleasure are intimately linked. Pleasure springs from satisfied desire, a desire that has attained its object or its good. Man, a being who desires, is thus oriented towards or made for pleasure — the maximum pleasure. The aim of Aristotelian ethics is to help human beings choose the activity from which they will derive the greatest pleasure or joy, and thus become as happy as possible by divorcing themselves from activities that give them more superficial and temporary pleasure but prevent them from progressing towards the finest activities and pleasures.

Later, in Chapter 4, on the virtues, we shall see that this is not quite as simple a matter as it might at first appear. In fact, the baser, more immediate, easier pleasures can seduce a person and invade his field of consciousness to the point where he is prevented from orienting himself towards the nobler, greater, more ecstatic pleasures. Like the mountain climber, sometimes we have to take a bleak and difficult path in order to attain the joys of the summit, with all its sublime views. Happiness is also achieved at the price of a struggle.

But in every instance pleasure results from perfect activity and at the same time springs forth to perfect the act, because in the end things are experienced more intensely.

> *But the pleasure does not complete it* [an activity] *in the same way as the combination of object and sense, both good, just as health and the doctor are not in the same way the cause of a man's being healthy . . . Pleasure completes the activity not as the corresponding permanent state does, by its immanence, but as the end which supervenes as the bloom of youth does on those in the flower of their age.* (NE 1174b23–25 and 32–34)

Let us say that pleasure completes or crowns the act, in the way that beauty comes with youth. And just as a ripe fruit is attractive to see and stimulates the appetite, so pleasure augments the goodness of the act and heightens desire. The pleasure resulting from activity gives spice to life; it makes us conscious of our existence; it then becomes the pleasure of existing. We should not make the mistake, however, of thinking that pleasure is the end, for the end is the act itself. Rather, pleasure is given when the end is fully attained, as a bonus or consequential end. It is given gratuitously; as soon as we want to grasp it for its own sake, or touch it, it fades — or ensnares us. The moment we turn away from the object to savour the pleasure alone, we loose sight of the object. By virtue of this fact, the activity, the union of object and subject, becomes less intense, and so too does the pleasure. The only way to recoup the latter is to find ever more exciting objects. This seems to be true of the pleasures of love, too. When we seek pleasure without really loving the person, we grow tired even of the pleasure and begin to experience the need to change partners. When we love the pleasure without loving the person, the pleasure itself fades away.

This is where Aristotelian analysis contrasts starkly not only with our contemporary culture, but also with other analytical thought prevalent among the ancient Greeks. I am thinking in particular of that of Epicurus, whose writings appeared twenty years after Aristotle.

The philosophy of pleasure in Epicurus should be understood on the basis of his pessimism, especially with regard to desire. For Epicurus, desire was a source of torment because of the restlessness that lay at its roots. The task of philosophy, which purports to be medicine for the soul, is to resolve this invasion of desire. It does so first by limiting our desires. Hence the famous distinction between *natural* desires and *vain* desires, then, in the case of natural desires, between those that are absolutely necessary and the others. Only those that are natural and necessary should always be satisfied, and those that are natural and not necessary only sometimes. In any case, the mastered desire will be fully extinguished and resolved only by the pleasure that is its conclusion and end.

Let us be clear about this: What Epicurus called pleasure is the *quietude* that follows the appeasement of desire. Also, when on several occasions he declares "pleasure to be the beginning and end of the blessed life," he is not inviting us to indulge in debauchery. He means that the soul has attained its end when it is at peace, for pleasure and peace are one and the same thing. That is where he differs radically from Aristotle, who sites pleasure in activity.

Is this just a nicety of philosophical approach? Or does it not, rather, represent a profound difference with regard to how we should approach life? It is one thing to seek happiness in thrilling, ecstatic, vital activity, as Aristotle advocates. It is quite another to conceive of happiness as the absence of pain, or *ataraxie*, as Epicurus does. This doctrine of *ataraxie* has been compared to Buddhist wisdom, but the resemblance is only a tenuous one. For the serenity that Epicurus seeks is not nirvana and the idea of renouncing the illusion of the Self found in Eastern philosophy remains alien to the Greek soul.[1]

Epicurus may well regard pleasure as an end, but he differs from our contemporary culture in that he never invites us to overindulge. After a period of repression, we have witnessed today a powerful return to the vindication of pleasure. A swinging back of the pendulum may be appropriate, but it is one that seems to carry us very much further than we really want. The frantic rushing about in all directions in pursuit of pleasure is harmful to us. And here again, Aristotle's thinking is pertinent to our time.

The Culture of Pleasure

In its most common form, man uses pleasure as relaxation, as a remedy for stress. Pleasure is like a breath of fresh air in a life consumed by tension and worry. The human being in pain needs to pause for breath. Aristotle calls this *curative pleasure.*

> *Owing to the excesses of pain that men experience, they pursue excessive and in general bodily pleasure as being a cure for the pain. Now curative agencies produce intense feeling — which is the reason why they are pursued — because they show up against the contrary pain.* (NE 1154a30)

Aestheticism is a doctrine that promotes pleasure in another, somewhat refined form involving mastery of sensibility for the purposes of enhanced enjoyment. This doctrine was superbly conveyed by Oscar Wilde in *The Picture of Dorian Gray.* It is a question of curing the soul by the senses, as Lord Henry explains to Dorian, but still remaining in control. Anything goes: the pleasures of the arts, of love, etc., but without man being reduced to the bestial. The refined man learns to defer pleasure in the interests of greater enjoyment.

We all seek pleasure as a means of escaping the hardships of our existence. We cannot bear conflict, solitude, the difficulties of life, especially those of relationships. We seek the remedy in instant pleasure, which, by gratifying our affectivity, lifts us out of our sadness for a while. We indulge in an incalculable number of such pleasures, often bodily pleasures or those likely to have an immediate impact on our mood: the gratification of food, possessions, relationships, those passing friendships, for example, that last as long as we are getting on well together and are dropped as soon as they become wearisome. These instant pleasures are ones that do not endure, unless we push them to excess, as in the case of drug addiction.

The abuse of drugs is rooted in evasion of reality taken to the extreme. The drugged state is often even expressed in terms of a journey. There are good and bad "trips" and those from which there is no return. The person on drugs refuses to combat or even confront reality, finding it too bleak and too painful. Contact with this reality causes him too much anguish and gives rise to a feeling of impotence. Chemical substances cause the drug user to experience powerful emotions that make him feel that he exists, as seventeen-year-old Loïc tells a newspaper: "I like being on drugs, feeling good. . . .You dance like crazy all night, you are the music. If you smoke, you're Zen, but the energy isn't there, your body doesn't follow. Now everyone's taking faster and faster stuff. You go to gigs, you take a trip — no worries, a tablet you can swallow in one go. You can pick up a hell of a lot of drugs quite cheaply . . . Ecstasy, getting high, raves — when you get into that world, you want to stay there. It's powerful, it's a bunch of young people, no one tries to get in your head. You take drugs, help each other. Just being among young people, it's wild. For a year and a half I took nothing but E. I fell into the trap too quickly. After E I wanted to try cocaine; it's so great when it goes okay. I have a twin brother studying for his school-leaving exams. We don't live in the same world."

The ancient Greeks did not have substances such as Ecstasy or heroin at their disposal. They were nevertheless capable of monstrous enough orgies combining excesses of food and drink with sexuality. Aristotle knew well what energy man could direct against himself in the search for pleasure. Even in his time, he noticed that

> . . . *most men, and men of the most vulgar type seem (not without some ground) to identify the good, or happiness with pleasure; which is the reason why they love the life of enjoyment . . . Now the mass of mankind are evidently quite slavish in their tastes, preferring a life suitable to beasts, but they get some ground for their view from the fact that many of those in high places share the tastes of Sardanapallus.*[2] (NE 1095b15–23)

He also noted that bodily pleasures often took precedence over other, higher ones, those of the soul or mind.

> *But the bodily pleasures have appropriated the name* [of pleasure] *both because we oftenest steer our course for them and because all men share in them; thus because they alone are familiar, men think there are no others.* (NE 1153b34–35)

Drug abuse is the perfect example of a bodily pleasure taken to the point of paroxysm. It belongs to the same line of logic as the frenzied eating and drinking that ultimately ignore other forms of pleasure. Young Loïc lets us see that he does not know the pleasure of study: "I have a twin brother studying for his school-leaving exams. We don't live in the same world."

This kind of experience is also too restrictive really to be happiness. It sucks us into the need for repeated consummation and deprives us of our liberty. The truly happy person is, on the contrary, creative and free. His or her experience of pleasure is quite different. It springs from human perfection and not from some chemical artifice. It is more lasting and finer. Socrates knew how to enjoy the pleasures of the table just as well as, if not better than, those most accustomed to them, and yet he also knew how to fast and did not lose control of himself. The drugged state, on the other hand, is experienced as an evasion of one's self, and the pleasure that accompanies it as an escape from reality. Life is too hard, loneliness is unbearable and effort beyond our reach, and so we flee. This flight can culminate in a form of suicide. It is an experience that has nothing to do with the pleasure born of an encounter with reality and of harmony with it.

The trap into which Loïc has fallen is that of having taken the quest for pleasure to be an end. And now his pursuit of pleasure has ensnared and holds him. The margin left to him is a narrow one: He can avoid taking two tablets instead of one in order to "stay high" and never come back down, like one of his friends, who is now handicapped.

Another trend in our culture links the experience of pleasure even more radically to that of omnipotence. There is nothing more guaranteed to make me feel my own power than transgressing prohibitions. I feel stronger than the law, stronger than God. Jean-Claude Guillebaud showed, in his book *La Tyrannie du plaisir*,[3] how May 1968[4] furthered this culture of pleasure linked to transgression. There is a logical progression from *enjoying uninhibitedly* to *transgressing in order to enjoy.* Hence all kinds of transgressions: heterosexual, homosexual, and incestuous.

Once the sexual revolution had occurred, other areas of transgression had to be found. Now the phenomenon of vandalism is more widespread, together with an ever more radical desire to transgress even to the point of murder. A total enjoyment of extreme violence is demonstrated by the sorry example of soccer hooligans. The words of an Englishman in the *Football Factory* give an insight into such an experience: "We approach the stadium. I am burning up inside. The excitement is still there; I can feel my whole body vibrating. It may sound strange but it's true. It's better even than making love to a woman or driving at full speed . . . I can already hear the murmur of the crowd inside and the Chelsea supporters' song being sung over and over again. This is the life . . . Then I have a block of reinforced concrete in my hand — there is a piece of iron sticking right through the middle of it — and there we are running down the street and I hear it, a unique sound, a buzz that comes from somewhere deep inside me when the pressure's on." He goes on to attack a man who eventually dies from the assault. And then our hooligan moves on to something else . . . Like young Loïc, he is seeking the powerful emotion that he calls a "*buzz*" or even "*life.*" He loves violence to the point of criminal insanity for the sensation it gives him. He too is making the quest for enjoyment an end in itself.

This passion for pleasure, which is so characteristic of a large part of our contemporary culture, seems to me to be both a limitation and an advantage.

On the one hand, this diversion of our culture into the pursuit of pleasure as an end in itself appears to me a blind alley as far as the experience of pleasure itself is concerned. Repeated consummation kills pleasure. It has no respect for the period of desire. Yet the man who is really able to enjoy pleasure is the one who knows *how* to desire. Desire and reason are not opposites — quite the reverse. The better I know how to distinguish between pleasures, the more my desire is heightened.

Never before has so little been made of desire as today. It is as if an entire generation had lost its appetite! The pursuit of pleasure as the sole end concludes with a loss of interest in the object. "It doesn't matter whether it's on cocaine or Ecstasy, so long as I get high," the young drug addict tells himself! Desire, on the other hand, is an opening up to the object. In as much as pleasure is a matter of fusion, so desire is oriented towards the object. What we need then to restore is a culture of desire, that is, if we wish to be restored to life.

The advantage of our passion for pleasure exists at the level of education. Today it is difficult to educate people simply on the basis of law, but it can be done, using pleasure as a starting point. Pleasure is an indication of what gives enjoyment and attracts, of a profound conformity between object and subject. In the case of adults with mental handicaps, such as the people we welcome at l'Arche, where I have been living for over thirty years, it is impossible to start with law. If, however, we find out what it is that people enjoy, be it music, a walk in the woods, or the discovery of an object, we can awaken a desire and help them move towards the object of their desire. What is true of a person with a mental handicap, even a profound one, is true also of children and, indeed, of every one of us. Even when I place myself outside any considerations of morality, I experience pleasure, provided there is an equivalence between what I am and the object. If there is this equivalence, I desire it: It is my good. And when I find it I blossom, I am overwhelmed with pleasure.

There can be no education if we do not recognize the place of pleasure. Pleasure can play this educational role, however, only if it is accompanied by structures and laws. It is not a question of indulging the child or adolescent in his wants, but of understanding what attracts him and his way of functioning, and leading him to something more profound, towards other experiences of pleasure. Take a young man who has no inner structure, but who derives much pleasure from music. We might perhaps suggest that he learn the guitar, and if he enjoys it, to take lessons. Thus motivated, he can then progress and become disciplined, properly directed towards his end: being able to play well. Pleasure leads him, through a certain structuring of his being, towards the greater pleasure of playing and being applauded for his success.

Once again, for Aristotle, pleasure is defined by the activity, which is itself determined by its object. There is no distinction for him between joy and pleasure. There is not, on the one hand, egotistical and carnal pleasure and on the other, spiritual, intellectual, and altruistic joy. All activity, noble or otherwise, is accompanied by pleasure. The same word, *hedone*, is used to denote both the pleasure of study and the pleasure of eating or drinking. There are as many forms of pleasure as there are types of activity.

It is the value of the object pursued that determines the intensity and depth of pleasure.

Aristotle's insight that pleasure is not the end, but the fruit, of activity is one of value for our times. Today we want pleasure without attaining the object that is best suited to our humanity. Here Aristotle helps us to rehabilitate both desire and pleasure. Pleasure cannot be divorced from its foundation, that vital activity that presupposes a conformity between the subject and his object.

Friendship

Friendship is the other axis of the profoundly human moral science propounded by Aristotle. In fact, without Aristotle saying so explicitly, it is possible to identify a link between friendship and pleasure. The latter is not desired for itself, it is a bonus end, the fruit of activity. Friendship is also a fruit, that of virtue. It makes the virtuous life particularly pleasant.

Friendship is simultaneously what is most necessary in life and what is greatest in man: "The justice that is most just seems to belong to friendship" (NE 1155a27).[5]

Cicero, who had read Aristotle, uses an appealing metaphor: "To take friendship out of life is to take the sun away from the world,"[6] an idea dear to the *Nichomachean Ethics*: "For without friends no one would choose to live" (NE 1155a3).

> *Surely it is strange, too, to make the supremely happy man a solitary, for no one would choose the whole world on condition of being alone, since man is a political*[7] *creature and one whose nature is to live with others.* (NE 1169b17–19)

And in poverty and in other misfortunes men think friends are the only refuge. It helps the young, too, to keep from error; it aids older people by ministering to their needs and supplementing the activities that are failing from weakness; those in the prime of life it stimulates to noble actions — "two going together" — for with friends men are more able both to think and to act. (NE 1155a11–16)

Aristotle stretches the definition of friendship considerably to mean sharing, life together, communion. "His friend is another self" (NE 1166a31); that is why in friendship we "rejoice and grieve" together (NE 1171a5). And Aristotle cites with respect the opinions of those who maintain that friendship consists of a life in common, in the making of the same choices, or in the sharing of the same pain and joy. "All the proverbs, too, agree with this, e.g. 'a single soul,' and 'what friends have is common property' and 'friendship is equality'"(NE 1168b8).

Justice renders us open to respect for others. Friendship goes further. Nothing pushes us quite as radically beyond ourselves as friendship. So far, we have spoken of happiness as a subjective and solitary activity that involves an attitude of openness to the world but that makes the subject alone responsible for and the beneficiary of his own perfection. With friendship we see another dimension emerge, giving a new slant to happiness.

We have all, however, experienced setbacks in friendship, as if we had difficulty being true to our relationships. Aristotle considers this in detail. Why is it that we are sometimes let down by our friends? Why do some of our friendships not stand the test of time? How are we to know whether what binds us to our friend is really solid and authentic? All these questions lead him to differentiate between several forms of friendship. Not all of them are authentic.

The Beginning of Friendship: Goodwill

Friendship is in the same vein as goodwill, Aristotle tells us at the outset. Unlike simple *attachment*, which may just as readily be concerned with objects, goodwill is directed towards other human beings. Something is awakened in us with regard to someone else — a kind of interest. Why? Because we have perceived in him "some excellence." This may be quite superficial, such as when we support an athlete. He seems the best to us and we would like him to win. Or it may be more profound, such as when we have seen something precious in another person: his inner beauty, one might say. Montaigne[8] thus speaks of his encounter with his friend "La Boétie" as an "inner attraction of one human being to another, of one soul to another."

> *In general, goodwill arises on account of some excellence and worth, when one man seems to another beautiful or brave or something of the sort, as we pointed out in the case of competitors in a contest.* (NE 1167a18–20)

The attraction at the root of goodwill is not to be confused with that which is the beginning of love, nor with an attraction of the heart, nor with a desire to make up for solitude or to fill a void. It is an attraction that depends upon *virtue*. We have seen another's excellence and we feel benevolently towards him, as the etymology of the Latin *benevolentia* (from *bene-volare*, to wish well) suggests. But we are not yet ready to commit ourselves to him.

> *Goodwill is not even friendly feeling. For it does not involve intensity or desire, whereas these accompany friendly feeling; and friendly feeling implies intimacy while goodwill may arise of a sudden, as it does towards competitors in a contest; we come to feel goodwill for them and to share in their wishes, but we would not do anything with them.* (NE 1166b33–67a3)

> *Goodwill seems, then, to be a beginning of friendship, as the pleasure of the eye is the beginning of love . . . so too it is not possible for people to be friends if they have not come to feel goodwill for each other. . . . And so one might by an extension of the term friendship say that goodwill is inactive friendship, though when it is prolonged and reaches the point of intimacy it becomes friendship.* (NE 1167a3–14)

To become friendship, goodwill must be *reciprocal* and *recognized*.

> *But to those who thus wish good we ascribe only goodwill if the wish is not reciprocated; goodwill when it is reciprocal being friendship. Or must we add "when it is recognized"? For many people have goodwill to those whom they have not seen but judge to be good or useful; and one of these might return this feeling. These people seem to bear goodwill to each other; but how could one call them friends when they do not know their mutual feelings?* (NE 1155b32–1156a3)

Reciprocal goodwill must therefore be extended into some form of life together:

> But those who have regard for one another, and yet do not live their lives together, seem to have goodwill rather than to be friends. For nothing is so characteristic of friends as sharing their lives. (NE 115b18 – 20)[9]

This life together consists first in joining in the vital activities that are of most interest to the two friends. It is these activities that form the bond between them, even if this bond is only superficial.

> For friendship is a partnership, and as a man is to himself, so he is to his friend; now in his own case the consciousness of his being is desirable, and so therefore is the consciousness of his friend's being, and the activity of this consciousness is produced when they live together, so that it is natural that they aim at this. And whatever existence means for each class of men, whatever it is for whose sake they value life, in that they wish to occupy themselves with their friends; and so some drink together, others dice together, others join in athletic exercises and hunting, or in the study of philosophy, each class spending their days together in whatever they love most in life. (NE 1171b32–1172a7)

This is where we see friendship distance itself from the sentiment of lovers. "She loves me? She loves me not?" the man in love is constantly asking himself, without really wanting to know the answer. Love delights in fantasy and feeds on it. In true friendship we are less troubled.

Friendship seeks reciprocity and moves more readily to the point of recognition. We have to "dare to make an approach and make contact," as Montaigne again tells us, otherwise we remain in a state of wishful thinking. Friendship is primarily a life together that is nourished by shared activity and not by dreams about the other person.

Mutual and reciprocal goodwill is the inner attitude of our affectivity, or heart, which disposes us to friendship, and is one fundamental aspect of it.

But how are to be sure that what we are dealing with is true friendship? That we are really centred on the other person and not on ourselves? That we are not becoming bogged down in a lazy friendship? That we are not, with a greater or lesser degree of subtlety, dominating the other person? A good way to check the authenticity of our friendship is through an experience of crisis. Often this reveals the hidden dimensions of what binds friends together.

In Times of Crisis

We may well believe that we are true friends, but when a crisis occurs, it is often catastrophic, revealing the true nature of the relationship that unites us! We may then realize that we did not really matter to the other person, that we have been used. We may be disappointed and swear that we will never be caught out like that again — so long as it was not we who, subtly, did the manipulating. Either way, the friendship is put to the test.

Any crisis is an opportunity for friendship. As with anything that is living, it is a chance for clarification and progress.

Another question that arises is whether friendships should or should not be broken off when the other party does not remain the same. Perhaps we may say that there is nothing strange in breaking off a friendship based on utility or pleasure, when our friends no longer have these attributes. . . . But one might complain of another if, when he loved us for our usefulness or pleasantness, he pretended to love us for our character. For, as we said at the outset, most differences arise between friends when they are not friends in the spirit in which they think they are. (NE 1165a37–b8)

Here Aristotle provides us with some very interesting criteria for discernment. He distinguishes between three sorts of friendship: true friendship centred on the good of the other, which is fully deserving of the name of friendship; friendship based on what is pleasant; and friendship based on usefulness. These are the three motives that can inspire friendship.

For not everything seems to be loved but only the lovable, and this is good, pleasant, or useful. (NE 1155b18)

Now these reasons [what is good, pleasant, or useful] *differ from each other in kind; so, therefore, do the corresponding forms of love and friendship. There are therefore three kinds of friendship, equal in number to the things that are lovable; for with respect to each there is a mutual and recognized love, and those who love each other wish well to each other in that respect in which they love one another. Now those who love each other for their utility do not love each other for themselves but in virtue of some good which they get from each other. So too with those who love for the sake of pleasure; it is not for their character that men love ready-witted people, but because they find them pleasant. Therefore those who love for the sake of utility love for the sake of what is good for themselves, and those who love for the sake of pleasure do so for the sake of what is pleasant to themselves, and not in so far as the other is the person loved but in so far as he is useful or pleasant. And thus these friendships are only incidental; for it is not as being the man he is that the loved person is loved, but as providing some good or pleasure. Such friendships, then, are easily dissolved, if the parties do not remain like themselves; for if one party is no longer pleasant or useful, the other ceases to love him.* (NE 1156a5–20)

We have seen that Aristotle defined friendship by starting with the feeling experienced by the subject: mutual and reciprocal goodwill. Here he wonders about the aim of that feeling. Taking the end as his starting point, he invites us to greater understanding. What is it that, deep down, inspires my friendship? Is it the other person or I? There is something that can help us to know: the solidity of the relationship in time of crisis.

If a change of social status is enough to shatter a friendship, the relationship was not disinterested. The same is true if dishonour strikes one of my friends and I abandon him. Or again, if illness makes me reject someone whose company I really appreciated. I was not interested in the other person as another person but only insofar as he responded to my need, an affective need if I sought pleasure in his company, or simply gain, if he was useful to me.

Pleasure and utility are thus, for Aristotle, two ways of seeking one's own interests in a relationship. However, the egocentricity is more pronounced in one case than in the other:

> Of these two kinds that which is for the sake of pleasure is the more like friendship, when both parties get the same things from each other and delight in each other or in the same things, as in the friendships of the young; for generosity is more found in such friendships. Friendship based on utility is for the commercially minded. (NE 1158a18–22)

"Commercial mindedness" is found in a thousand and one forms in relationships, whether we are rich or poor, healthy or sick, young or old. Moreover, Aristotle draws our attention to the fact that, by creating an imbalance between people, inequality can tip a relationship in the direction of gain.

> Friendship for utility's sake seems to be that which most easily exists between contraries, e.g. between poor and rich, between ignorant and learned; for what a man actually lacks he aims at, and one gives something else in return. (NE 1159b13–15)

But it can also be a state of need that orients the relationship towards self-interest. If we expect the other person to give us something — protection, knowledge, affection — then does not provide it, we complain!

. . . the friendship of utility is full of complaints; for as they use each other for their own interests they always want to get the better of the bargain, and think they have got less than they should, and blame their partners because they do not get all they "want and deserve"; and those who do well by others cannot help them as much as those whom they benefit want. (NE 1162b17–20)

These are clashes that are well known to lovers, too:

. . . but in the friendship of lovers sometimes the lover complains that his excess of love is not met by love in return (though perhaps there is nothing lovable about him), while often the beloved complains that the lover who formerly promised everything now performs nothing. Such incidents happen when the lover loves the beloved for the sake of pleasure while the beloved loves the lover for the sake of utility . . . (NE 1164a2–7)

Friendship based on pleasure, for which Aristotle has the greater sympathy, is more likely to survive a crisis, because the presence of the other person is still central to the feeling. But the affectivity and the subjectivity involved at the forefront of this kind of relationship render this bond fragile, too. We have only to look at young people:

On the other hand the friendship of young people seems to aim at pleasure; for they live under the guidance of emotion, and pursue above all what is pleasant to themselves and what is immediately before them; but with increasing age their pleasures become different. This is why they quickly become friends and quickly cease to be so; their friendship changes with the object that is found pleasant, and such pleasure alters quickly. Young people are amorous too: for the greater part of the friendship of love depends on emotion and aims at pleasure; this is why they fall in love and quickly fall out of love, changing often within a single day. (NE 1156a32–b3)

This type of friendship can have its origins in a certain similarity: shared tastes, identical sensations, and similar activities that make the other person's company agreeable. We are thus very close to comradeship. It can also be fed by difference, by an exoticism that seduces and brings with it a breath of fresh air. Either way, this kind of relationship is subject to the hazards of its own subjectivity. When we no longer feel anything, what is left of the bond?

We are easily brought to the point of dissolving this form of friendship, but we are just as quickly able to bounce back with another. Like the culture of "surfing" that so enthralls our society, it is pleasurable but disruptive; our affectivity does not have the chance to mature. It stops at the *ego* stage, although in a different way from the pursuit of utility. In both cases, however, a relationship that cannot manage to be interested in the other person for him- or herself is a sign of immaturity. It is as if the ego remained blocked by the fundamental desire to be loved, to matter to someone, and to be everything to him. Aristotle, who did not have our human sciences at his disposal, subjects this tendency to close analysis:

Most people seem, owing to ambition, to wish to be loved rather than to love; which is why most men love flattery; for the flatterer is a friend in an inferior position,

*or pretends to be such and to love more than he is loved
. . . while those who desire honour from good men, and
men who know, are aiming at confirming their own
opinion of themselves; they delight in honour, therefore,
because they believe in their own goodness on the strength
of the judgement of those who speak about them. . . . But
it* [friendship] *seems to lie in loving rather than in being
loved.* (NE 1159a13–27)

It is easy to appreciate that friendship and maturity go
together. There comes a point when we must progress to
an active and generous love. Generosity is a quality that is
fashionable today, but the kind that goes with friendship
is not merely a generosity of service in which we want to
help the other person. That kind of generosity of feeling,
which can be close to pity, leaves the other person in a state
of inferiority, whereas "friendship is said to be equality"
(NE 1157b35). Aristotle frequently identifies himself with
this ancient Greek principle. If we cannot manage to see in
the person we are helping a certain human excellence or
inner beauty that is attractive, if we do not experience joy
in her presence, we cannot speak of friendship.

With this reflection on friendships based on resemblance, we can now move on to broach what makes for
perfect friendship.

Perfect Friendship

It is to be hoped that true friendship is not subject to the
same defects as inferior forms of friendship. We are not
likely to complain about a true friend, for instance,
because we are not assessing him primarily on what he

brings us. "I recognize friendship by the fact that it cannot be disappointed," Saint-Exupéry tells us, "but what you do with the person you love is promptly turn him into a slave, and if he does not assume the burdens of that slavery, you condemn him for it."[10] Nor is true friendship dissolved at the first difficulty encountered. It knows how to withstand trials and even finds in them an opportunity for growth. "I love the friend who is faithful in temptation [again these are Saint-Exupéry's words] for if there is no temptation there is no fidelity and I have no friend." From where does true friendship derive this solidity? Is it not from the fact that, entirely desirous as it is of the other person's good, it is less subject to the fluctuations of enjoyment or the pursuit of profit? "In true friendship," Montaigne tells us this time, "I give myself to my friend more than I seek to pull him to me."[11]

Therein lies the entire difference: Instead of being centred on "me," the friendship is centred on the other person, his life and his good, and on a sharing of the same values that are pursued together.

> For (1) we define a friend as one who wishes and does what is good, or seems so, for the sake of his friend, or (2) as one who wishes his friend to exist and live, for his sake. . . . (NE 1166a3–5)

In true friendship, everything, will and feelings alike, is oriented by this concern for the other person.

> We may describe friendly feeling towards any one as wishing for him what you believe to be good things, not for your own sake but for his, and being inclined, so far as you

can, to bring these things about. A friend is one who feels thus and excites these feelings in return: those who think they feel thus towards each other think themselves friends. This being assumed, it follows that your friend is the sort of man who shares your pleasure in what is good and your pain in what is unpleasant, for your sake and for no other reason. (Rhet. 1380b35–1381a6)

Friendship includes tenderness, such as a mother's love for her child. Aristotle actually likens love that gives priority to the other person to maternal feeling: ". . . as one who wishes his friend to exist and live, for his sake; which mothers do to their children" (NE 1166a6). And how could I not feel tenderness for a person in whom I recognize fine qualities or inner beauty, and who pursues the same values or interests as I do? For this is the reason for friendship: I have seen the goodness, the beauty of another person and have been attracted by it. We have the same understanding of the meaning of life and existence.

Who is capable of loving in this way? The man who has a sense of what is human and what are properly human activities, the man with an enlightened mind and upright will, the man who is not jealous of his friend, who is open to the other person — that is to say, the virtuous or good man.

Perfect friendship is the friendship of men who are good, and alike in virtue; for these wish well alike to each other qua good, and they are good in themselves. Now those who wish well to their friends for their sake are most truly friends; for they do this by reason of their own nature and not incidentally; therefore their friendship lasts as long as they are good — and goodness is an enduring thing. (NE 1156b6–11)

How can I lay claim to friendship if, in me "wishing well" is just an emotion? Once the emotion has been swept away, there will be nothing left. And if I am still in a state of immaturity, trapped in my ego, swayed by my passions, how can I be open to another person and give priority to what is good for him, over my own interests? The solidity of the bond derives from something deep within us that is other than emotion. It stems from the intimate disposition of the soul to choose, skillfully and joyfully, what is good for the other person.

. . . but mutual love [friendship] *involves choice and choice springs from a state of character;*[12] *and men wish well to those whom they love, for their sake, not as a result of feeling but as a result of a state of character.* (NE 1157b31)

Friendship requires this inner stability in a person, an inner structure or state of character that Aristotle calls *virtue.* The virtues are intellectual or moral qualities that steer the will, the capacity to judge and engage one's freedom for another person's good. The birth and deepening of these virtues takes time and exercise — disposition *results* from exercise, Aristotle likes to tell us. It is what the fox wishes to teach the prince in Saint-Exupéry's *The Little Prince*[13]: "If you want a friend, then win me over." He at once places friendship in a long-term perspective and marks it out with rites that structure the time. Thus the little prince must come every day at the same hour so that he has time to "clothe his heart." With no less effect and lyricism, Aristotle too emphasizes that

> . . . *it is natural that such friendships* [those based on goodness] *should be infrequent; for such men are rare. Further, such friendship requires time and familiarity; as the proverb says, men cannot know each other till they have "eaten salt together"; nor can they admit each other to friendship or be friends till each has been found lovable and been trusted by each. Those who quickly show the marks of friendship to each other wish to be friends, but are not friends unless they both are lovable and know the fact; for a wish for friendship may arise quickly, but friendship does not.* (NE 1156b25–32)

Friendship is thus a pinnacle of life realized in the pursuit of, the desire for, what is good for a friend.

> . . . *those who are friends on the ground of virtue are anxious to do well by each other (since that is a mark of virtue and of friendship), and between men who are emulating each other in this there cannot be complaints or quarrels; no one is offended by a man who loves him and does well by him — if he is a person of nice feeling he takes his revenge by doing well by the other. And the man who excels the other in the services he renders will not complain of his friend, since he gets what he aims at; for each man desires what is good.* (NE 1162b6–13)

True love, that of authentic friends, is also a love that is active — a dynamic, enterprising love. Desiring what is good for another person does not mean simply being well disposed towards him and really open to him, but also being willing to expend oneself for and with him. Doing good together — that is what makes us fully friends. Love sees on a large scale and is inseparable from the experience of what is good. I want for my friend the greatest goods: not simply good health or success in business, but fullness of life. But then, what makes us fully alive? That which best nourishes the soul: the pursuit of truth culminating in contemplation, and devoting our lives to our fellow citizens through acts of justice. We can do this alone, but when there are two, we do it with even more enthusiasm and joy. The charisma of friendship, its particular grace, is to render the exercise of virtue even more pleasant. For it is easier to seek the ultimate truths when there are two of you, by exchanging ideas with one another and mutually enlightening one another.

> *Now if he were a solitary, life would be hard for him; for by oneself it is not easy to be continuously active; but with others and towards others it is easier. With others therefore his activity will be more continuous.* (NE 1170a4–7)

That is why what drives the dynamic of friendship is living together. "For there is nothing so characteristic of friends as living together" (NE 1157b20). This life together is at the heart of friendship, its essential element. Life together does not mean mere cohabitation, "as in the case of cattle, feeding in the same place," as Aristotle puts it (NE 1170b14). It is a life lived in communion, that is nourished by shared actions with a view to great and noble things. It is sharing the same vision of things, the same tastes, the same understanding of life; it implies actions or projects carried out together, especially the ones that are closest to our hearts. Friendship is all the better for engaging in acts that are noble and great. It is, above all else, the desire for those beautiful and noble actions and their realization that cements friendship; it is they that give meaning to the bond. If the time spent together is reduced, if what friends possess is no longer held in common (see EN 1168b8 on page 55), the friendship itself is likely to be diminished.

> . . . *if the absence is lasting, it seems actually to make men forget their friendship; hence the saying "out of sight, out of mind."* (NE 1157b12)

Friends seek each other out not to look at one another, notes Saint-Exupéry, but to embark together on those activities that they consider to be the centre and the end of their lives. Cicero also refers to the union between friends when he has Lelius say, "Scipio and I were united in the same public and private activities, united at home both in peacetime and in war, and between us there existed what makes the powerful bond of friendship: a perfect accord of wills, tastes and feelings."[14]

It is also through this life together that I communicate best in my friend's existence. In a very dense and powerful text, Aristotle develops this idea of communion. Through friendship I communicate in the consciousness that my friend has of his own existence. For in the same way that we feel that we are alive and exist through activity and derive pleasure from it, so, through friendship, we feel our friend live and exist. And the union is so profound that the goodness of the life of our friend extends to us and gives us pleasure. In friendship there is almost a communion, a merging of two beings and their rightful good. The friend is an *other self.* Everything that I experience, he experiences.

> *. . . and if as the virtuous man is to himself, he is to his friend also (for his friend is another self): if all this be true, as his own being is desirable for each man, so, or almost so is that of his friend. Now his being was seen to be desirable because he perceived his own goodness, and such perception is pleasant in itself. He needs, therefore, to be conscious of the existence of his friend as well, and this will be realized in their living together and sharing in discussion and thought; for this is what living together would seem to mean in the case of man, and not, as in the case of cattle, feeding in the same place.* (NE 1170b5–14)

The kind of friendship of Aristotle's intuition, and of his probable experience, falls perfectly in line with the aspirations of the Personalist philosophers, who seek authentic and deep interpersonal communication. In this friendship we continue to be two, but we are one in a great and noble activity that we accomplish together. Consciousness of the goodness of my friend fills me with just as much joy as if it were my own. My friend's happiness becomes my happiness.

So strong is this type of friendship that it is, of course, impossible to have a lot of friends.

> *. . . for it would seem actually impossible to be a great friend to many people. This is why one cannot love* [be in love with] *several people; love is ideally a sort of excess of friendship, and that can only be felt towards one person; therefore great friendship too can only be felt towards a few people.* (NE 1171a10–13)

Equality and Inequality

Perfect friendship of the kind that Aristotle describes implies equality of the two friends: equality in value, equality in status. This is something that is perfectly realized when two people of equal virtue perform fulfilling and noble activities together. But is friendship possible when a relationship involves inequality? When one party is superior to the other?

> *But there is another kind of friendship, viz. that which involves an inequality between the parties, e.g. that of father to son and in general of elder to younger, that of man to wife[15] and in general that of ruler to subject. . . . Each party, then, neither gets the same from the other, nor ought to seek it; but when children render to parents what they ought to render to those who brought them into the world, and parents render what they should to their children, the friendship of such persons will be abiding and excellent.* (NE 1158b12–24)

It is then possible to build a friendship on a basis of inequality, provided we do not deny this inequality from the outset. On the contrary, by recognizing it, we can make the bond between us strong and true. We can even re-establish a form of equality, an equality that is proportional.

> *In all friendships implying inequality, the love also should be proportional, i.e. the better should be more loved than he loves . . . for when the love is in proportion to the merit of the parties, then in a sense arises equality, which is certainly held to be characteristic of friendship.* (NE 1158b23–28)

Further on, Aristotle returns to the case of men and women, or married couples. Unequal, in his eyes, in status, their friendship remains of an inferior order. But within their particular parameters, they can go a long way towards true friendship.

> *. . . both utility and pleasure seem to be found in this kind of friendship. But this friendship may be based also on virtue, if the parties are good; for each has his own virtue and they will delight in the fact.* (NE 1162a24–26)

This friendship between unequal partners is also to be found between the master and the slave, who, as far as Aristotle is concerned, is a "living tool" within the family.

> Qua [as a] *slave then, one cannot be friends with him. But* qua [as a] *man one can.* (NE 1161b6–7)

Friendship and the Fullness of Human Life

We have clearly seen that friendship desires what is good for the other person. Perfect friendship also carries the love of one's self to completion and does not try to suppress it. Aristotle raises the question of whether the good man is an egoist. Of course he is, he says, because he desires his own perfection, his own goodness, and his own most perfect accomplishment. Thus he is thinking of himself. But he is very different from an egoist in the usual sense of the word, that is to say, someone who is closed in upon himself, seeking his own pleasure. Aristotle goes on to speak very beautifully of friendship:

It is true of the good man too that he does many acts for the sake of his friends and his country, and if necessary dies for them; for he will throw away both wealth and honours and in general the goods that are objects of competition, gaining for himself nobility. . . . he would prefer a short period of intense pleasure to a long one of mild enjoyment, a twelve-month of noble life to many years of humdrum existence, and one great and noble action to many trivial ones. Now those who die for others doubtless attain this result. . . . it is therefore a great prize that they choose for themselves. They will throw away wealth too on condition that their friends will gain more; for while a man's friend gains wealth he himself achieves nobility; he is therefore assigning the greater good to himself. The same too is true of honour and office; all these things he will sacrifice to his friend; for this is noble and laudable for himself. Rightly then is he thought to be good, since he chooses nobility before all else. But he may even give up actions to his friends; it may be nobler to become the cause of his friend's acting than to act himself. (NE 1169a17–34)

In the following chapters, we shall talk about the great and noble activities that enable us to become perfectly accomplished. The activities that Aristotle describes as virtuous — because they stem from a stable inner disposition — can sometimes appear arduous: being courageous, temperate, generous, etc., but they are easier when shared with friends. That is why Aristotle tells us that "*. . . if he were a solitary, life would be hard for him*" (NE 1170a5).

CHAPTER 3

THE HUNGER FOR TRUTH

What is the highest activity? For Aristotle, the quest for happiness is linked to this question. By "highest activity" we are meant to understand the finest, most sublime activity, the one that is going to enable us to progress furthest in the development of our humanity. It is also the activity that is the final end of all others, the keystone of all our searching and desires. It is the most unifying activity, the one that unites all our capacities and potencies by raising their orientation.

This "highest activity" has yet to be actually defined, which may seem surprising, given all that has already been said about happiness, virtue, and friendship — especially friendship, for which our contemporary society has a preference. We may think spontaneously that we find our deepest fulfillment in a relationship with another person, in the encounter with another person. Aristotle also considered this possibility. Why else would he have elaborated so extensively on friendship in Books 8 and 9 of his *Ethics*? But, as we have already established, he did not conceive friendship to be an end in itself. In friendship it is not enough just to carry on living with another person and deriving pleasure from him. Friendship is a form of communion that is open to something other than itself. Friendship is being together while still tending towards the pursuit of the same good. There remains the choice of what good should be pursued together. Two great aims are available to friends: the pursuit of justice in the city-state and the pursuit of truth.

The *pursuit of justice,* which I shall deal with in the next chapter — doing good together, organizing society for the greatest benefit of all — is indeed a great and noble activity, and all the more so for the fact that we rely on our friends in order to achieve it and that they in turn on us. The *pursuit of truth* — seeking to understand all things in terms of their most fundamental causes — is a more solitary choice in life, but there again, pursuing it with friends brings greater happiness. Aristotle makes no secret of the fact that he prefers this latter activity because it relates to what is more specific, noble, and divine in man. We have only to look at his own life and the choices he made. He went where his temperament as a seeker after truth took him. If we wish to know how the pursuit of truth can bring us to the pinnacle of happiness, there is no better way of finding out than by taking a detour and following Aristotle's own itinerary.

Aristotle's Life

So who was Aristotle? I would like to tell you, on the strength of what is known about his life, how I imagine him to have been, and how I imagine him to have led his life.

It seems to me that Aristotle, in his mature years, would have been one of those highly cultured men who knows how to listen, is passionately interested in reality, and is curious about everything there was to be discovered. Such men remain alert and attentive without being overwhelmed by information, because they have judgement. They know how to distinguish between what is true and what is false, what is essential and what is secondary. They know how to identify good intuitions. They are steady and open, capable of enthusiasm. They know how to join in the heat of the chase but also how to stop, be silent, look, and contemplate. They seek to unify their knowledge, to establish a unity within themselves. That is why they take time alone to meditate and internalize what they know, to weigh things up. They are less interested in the sum total of their knowledge than in having an accurate vision of the world, less interested in what people think of them than in the truth itself. I do not think it would be an exaggeration to say that Aristotle was cast somewhat in this mould, even though he was a kind of walking encyclopedia. Plato actually nicknamed him "the reader." Before reaching that stage, however, he had to make his way according to his particular talent.

When Aristotle arrived in Athens, he was a young man of seventeen. He was the son of Nichomachus (a name he would, in turn, give his own son, born of a second marriage), a doctor to the father of Philip of Macedon. What is more, Aristotle was later to return to the Macedonian court, invited by Philip to be his son Alexander's tutor. To what extent did Nichomachus, the father, influence Aristotle, the son? It is hard to say. Aristotle lost both his father and mother very early on in life, at the age of eleven. But one does not come from such a long line of doctors — the succession was handed down from father to son in his family — without inheriting something from it. There can be little doubt that Aristotle owes to his background his interest in reality, his passion for the living world, which he studied in all its aspects and even dissected, to the point where he became known as the "father of biology."

In Athens, his first master was Plato, a man with a very different temperament from his own. While Plato was inclined to venture into the sphere of pure contemplation, turning his back on sensible reality, Aristotle wanted to remain constantly in touch with the real. He loved all forms of experience, without ever short-circuiting what was sensible and down-to-earth. Ours is the "sub-lunar" world, he would later say, when elaborating on his cosmology. This world "beneath the moon" was the only one we had been called to inhabit.

For the time being, however, at the dawn of Aristotle's eighteenth year, we can imagine him under Plato's spell. Confronted with the various philosophical schools available in Athens — at least two at the time, not to mention the rhetors and other Sophists — Aristotle did not hesitate. He chose the Academy, which Plato had founded twenty years previously. In a city at the height of its intellectual effervescence, the school shone with particular brilliance. It was there that the seekers after truth who would become tomorrow's philosopher-kings were formed. There was an urgent need for such men, both from a philosophical perspective and from that of government of the city. Athens had fallen into the laxity of a democracy close to anarchy and needed fresh inspiration. In Plato's school, men learned to contemplate the "ideal city," precisely in order to apply their ideas on this earth.

Aristotle was more than interested; he was enthralled by the powerful inspiration of a master who was both brilliant and engaging. With Plato he learned about the thirst for truth and essential contemplation. He was to drink deeply at this spring. For twenty years, with eyes and ears wide open, he absorbed through every pore. Plato gave him an appetite for reflection, for understanding, and for following thought through to its limits in search of final causes. He exercised his mind in much the same way as an athlete does his muscles. Everything interested him: politics, human affairs, but also celestial things, nature, the stars. He threw himself into the quest for truth.

Plato, for his part, noticed Aristotle, referring to him not only as "the reader," but also "the thinking head," which was as good as calling him the brains of the school. Soon he made him his assistant. Aristotle did so well that he was put in charge of a course in rhetoric. He would stay at the Academy for twenty years, until Plato's death. And yet the disciple was not in complete agreement with his master, especially when it came to his approach to reality. For Plato, existing reality was deceptive. Politics had confirmed this for him when Athens, a city purportedly so enamoured of justice, had put to death "the most just of men," Socrates, who had not wanted to go along with a project of dubious honesty. Where then was true justice, a justice that was not deceptive? It was only visible to the eyes of the soul that wished to ascend from the visible world to the invisible world of Ideas. It was this contemplation of

the Idea, or the perfect model, of Justice — Justice *in itself,*
for its own sake — that could inspire just decisions. In
short, for Plato, true reality was not visible or "sensible"
reality, that is to say, as perceived by the senses. It was
beyond this world. It transcended it.

Aristotle came to a different conclusion. He was strongly
attracted to everything that went on in the material world.
He liked to touch it, dissect it. He was convinced that it was
possible to develop knowledge only by starting with what
was presented to our senses, to our touch, sight, hearing —
in short, our experience. He too wanted, indeed passionately, to come to a deep and ultimate understanding of
reality. He knew that it was not to be achieved only with
the eyes of the mind or the intelligence. But for him, the
effort of the mind — its tension, one might say — was an
attempt to penetrate what was material and visible, to gain
access to the heart of things, whereas for Plato that effort
consisted of turning away from sensible reality towards
what lay beyond the intelligible.

At what point did Aristotle distance himself from his
master? While he was still at the Academy? Later, when he
withdrew into a life of solitude? Or only when, having
become the master of a school in his turn, he attained his
full stature as a philosopher? Experts are still debating the
question. We know only that he tried Plato's dialectical
method; the few fragments of his *Socratic Dialogues* that
still exist bear witness to this. Yet, even in these early writings in which he imitates the man who was instructing
him, Aristotle is not completely in step with Plato. He is
already his own man. We know what it cost him to distance himself in this way, thanks to something he confides

in the *Nichomachean Ethics.* It appears discreetly, as an aside in Book 1, at the point where he is discussing precisely Plato's theses.

> *Yet it would perhaps be thought to be better, indeed to be our duty, for the sake of maintaining the truth even to destroy what touches us closely, especially as we are philosophers or lovers of wisdom; for, while both are dear, piety requires us to honour truth above our friends.* (NE 1096a13–17)

Aristotle made the search for truth the axis of his life. By entering the Academy he had opted for truth. In Plato's view there was no hope of becoming a good philosopher before the age of fifty, and you had to proceed to the truth *with your whole soul.* That is to say, you had to engage the best part of yourself, if not your entire being. "One should not show more respect for a man than for the truth," as he says in the *Republic.*

Upon the death of Plato, the situation resolved itself. Plato had achieved an advanced age, while Aristotle had reached full maturity as a man: he was thirty-eight. He might have taken over the running of the Academy, and perhaps given it a different emphasis, but that was not what happened. The Academy went to Speusippus, Plato's nephew. So Aristotle packed his bags and went his own way. He returned to nearer the Macedon of his origins, ending up on the island of Lesbos. There he became a man of the great outdoors and began to explore everything about him: fauna and flora but also the sky and its quasi-divine inhabitants, the stars.

The extraordinary abundance of life did not daunt

him; on the contrary, it fascinated him. His *History of Animals* shows him engaged in counting the number of gills in fish or enumerating the species of birds. He also scrutinized movements in the sky, to the point, it seems, of being able to predict the passing of a comet. Aristotle was an obstinate kind of man, obstinate in his determination to understand how the world functioned and where it was going. He took notes and classified what he observed, seeking to define as well as possible the articulations of observed reality. He kept a tight grip on fact in order to guard against straying into the imaginary. Aristotle distrusted the illusion that can accompany enthusiasm for certain theories.

> *For arguments about matters concerned with feelings and actions are less reliable than facts: and so when they clash with the facts of perception they are despised, and discredit the truth as well. . . . True arguments seem, then, most useful, not only with a view to knowledge, but with a view to life also; for since they harmonize with the facts they are believed, and so they stimulate those who understand them to live according to them.* (NE 1172a34–b7)

This is another point of difference between Aristotle and Plato who readily resorted to myth as an introduction to the contemplation of Ideas. Plato was a poet. He used the imagination to open up the intelligence. Aristotle's method was quite different. If he accumulated observations on every possible field — think of his extraordinary compendium of political constitutions, or his minutely detailed study of human character found further on in the *Ethics* — it was because he wanted to remain as close as possible to what things were. Things could not be known without contact, without touching — touching or touch underlay all the senses. Henri Bergson, a philosopher of our own time, had a good grasp of this process by which things are known in Aristotle: "It would be to extend the eye's vision by a vision of the mind. . . . It would be, by a powerful effort of mental vision, to pierce the material coating of things and read the formula that is invisible to the eye, that their material form unfolds and manifests."[1]

If things then present themselves to be seen, it is through contact with them, a contact that leads the intelligence to grasp, at a profound level, their intelligibility and their reason for being.

The Life of the Mind Lived to the Full

This detour into Aristotle's life sheds light on the direction in which we should seek happiness. Happiness can only be in the activity of that which is most extraordinary and noble in man, the activity of the intelligence.

> *Now that we have spoken of the virtues, the forms of friendship, and the varieties of pleasure, what remains is to discuss in outline the nature of happiness, since this is what we state the end of human nature to be. . . . We said, then, that it is not a disposition . . . we must rather class happiness as an activity.* (NE 1176a29–34)

> *If happiness is activity in accordance with virtue, it is reasonable that it should be in accordance with the highest virtue; and this will be that of the best thing in us. Whether it be reason or something else that is this element which is thought to be our natural ruler and guide*

and to take thought of things noble and divine . . . the activity of this in accordance with its proper virtue will be perfect happiness. That this activity is contemplative we have already said. (NE 1177a10–18)

Several points in this text require closer examination: the virtue in question is *wisdom,* the activity of which is contemplative or *theoretical,* as the Greek word states. We shall come back to this later. If wisdom is the highest virtue, it is because it comes to crown and perfect or, rather, to give life to and render actual what man bears within him, his capacity to go beyond what is sensible, visible, and finite, and to grasp the invisible and the infinite.

The Mind as the Best Thing in Us

Underlying Aristotle's explanation is also the conviction that "the best thing in us" relates to the mind. Intelligence, especially in its highest capacity — that of understanding a thing in its self — should be given the greatest importance.

Understanding is different from reasoning, discoursing, or arguing. It means rendering ourselves open to the thing itself, rather than pretending to master it through reasoning, establishing links, or classifying it. To understand is to connect with something in the intimacy of its being. We can do this only through an attitude that is simultaneously one of intellectual penetration and one of listening, active and passive at the same time. The mind works at grasping, beyond what is visible, that which forms the intelligible basis of the thing before it, until it connects through intuition. Intuition is the moment in which the *logos* (intelligence) makes contact with the *logos* (that which is intelligible in the thing). For everything, as we said in the first chapter, is illuminated from within by its intelligibility.

This faculty at the spearhead of the mind-*logos* — the intelligence that is apt to make contact with a thing in its intimate intelligibility — is what Aristotle calls the *nous*, and what Latin speakers would later call intelligence, insisting on the etymology of the term *intellectus*, "read within." Aristotle is full of admiration for this "noetic" capacity, which he finds in himself and in every man. There is nothing more "divine," nothing more "noble." And, at the same time, there is nothing more distinctively human.

> . . . *for even if it be small in bulk, much more does it in power and worth surpass everything. This would seem, too, to be each man himself, since it is the authoritative and better part of him. It would be strange, then, if he were to choose not the life of himself but that of something else . . . for man, therefore, the life according to reason is best and pleasantest, since reason more than anything else is man. This life therefore is also the happiest.* (NE 1178a1–9)

If we accept that, divorced from reason, there is no truly human or happy life, there is still work to be done, for contemplation involves the slow penetration of matter as described by Bergson. How do we start? By allowing the hunger for truth to arise in us again, and then by allowing ourselves to be penetrated, like the first philosophers or like children, by wonder.

The Hunger for Truth

If only we knew how to listen to our desires at their deepest level, we would find the hunger for knowledge and truth still there, intact. This is one of our mind's deepest aspirations. Anyone who seeks knows this from the amount of joy experienced when discoveries are made. We all, however, have within us this calling to be a seeker, a seeker of truth about ourselves and the world.

> *All men by nature desire to know. An indication of this is the delight we take in our senses; for even apart from their usefulness they are loved for themselves.* (Meta. 981a21)

Here Aristotle is pointing to a *gratuitous* desire for knowledge, a knowledge that is not justified in terms of its practical usefulness. It does not help us to run our homes better, or to build them, or to conduct our affairs. It is a knowledge that aims at nothing other than itself and which is like an inner light that brings joy. It is as if our intelligence finds its good and its joy in the simple fact of knowing, in the intelligibility of things. This, Aristotle tells us, is the sign of a deep aspiration of the mind.

If we observe children, we will find that they love to discover things and wonder at what they find. They admire things. It is important for us to retain this capacity to admire, to be seized by things, seized by their beauty. The tiniest child can teach us this. Children also ask surprising questions. "Often we hear words come out of the mouths of children, the meaning of which is deeply philosophical," writes Karl Jaspers, another philosopher of our time. "One child remarked with amazement, 'I am constantly trying to think that I am someone else, but I am still always me.'

He was touching on what is the origin of all certainty, the consciousness of being, through knowledge of oneself. He remained seized by the enigma of the self, an enigma that nothing can resolve. There he was, confronted by this limitation, wondering. Another, who had heard the story of Genesis —'In the beginning, God created the heaven and the earth' — immediately asked, 'So what was there before the beginning?'"[2]

The adult has often lost this "original capacity for wonder," which flows freely during childhood. The philosopher wants to rediscover it so that it can spring forth again.

Historically, the spirit of wonder is found at the very beginning of philosophy. The first Western philosophers had this attitude of wonder and admiration. That is what made them look at the world with new eyes. That was what enabled philosophical reflection to begin. Previously, people had been satisfied with profound mythological explanations. The mind had relied on and put its faith in history as recorded in myth.

Aristotle, who reread the history of philosophy in order to find his place in it, provides the following summary:

For it is owing to their wonder that men both now begin and at first began to philosophize; they wondered originally at the obvious difficulties about the greater matters, e.g. about the phenomena of the moon and those of the sun and of the stars, and about the genesis of the universe. And a man who is puzzled and wonders thinks himself ignorant . . . therefore since they philosophized in order to escape from ignorance, evidently they were pursuing science in order to know, and not for any utilitarian end. (Meta. 982b11–20)

Wonder and its attendant joy are sure indications of the happiness of knowing and understanding. True thinking begins with wonder. It is as if, before setting out on its route, the mind needs to stop at the things it is going to discover. This is the first dazzling experience pending the deeper wonder at the end of the journey, which Aristotle calls contemplation. It takes time before we reach this point, however. We have first to explore the real and its articulations. This is a process that requires much effort of mind and in which we can lose our way.

The investigation of the truth is in one way hard, in another easy. An indication of this is found in the fact that no one is able to attain the truth adequately. (Meta. 993a30)

On the other hand, Aristotle tells us, we do not fail completely.

It is just that we should be grateful, not only to those with whose views we may agree, but also to those who have expressed more superficial views. (Meta. 993b13)

Aristotle is a prudent and humble man. He does not rely on his own strengths alone but draws instead upon the efforts of thinkers who preceded him, that is to say, the first philosophers.

The Four Causes
For Aristotle, for his predecessors, and possibly for

philosophers of all time, the fundamental question remains: How do we attain reality? It seems more often to elude us than to reveal itself to us. It changes. As Heraclitus said, no sooner do we think we have grasped it than it has altered. He was not referring to man's inconstancy but to natural things, to the way that the daisy in bud today will bloom tomorrow and will ultimately fade. At what point is it stable? Never. In nature the only really stable law is that of *becoming.* But if things are always simultaneously *themselves* and *other* than themselves, in this incessant movement from genesis to decomposition, how are we to grasp them? How are we finally to grasp what it is that makes them what they are? How are we to understand the unity of a thing? Of the world? Of nature? What is it that makes up the unity of the world beyond the multifarious things it contains? The first philosophers, who were also observers, sought in nature the single substance at the base of all things. For some it was water, for others, fire or air.

> *Of the first philosophers, then, most thought the principles which were of the nature of matter were the only principles of all things. That of which all things that are consist, the first from which they come to be, the last into which they are resolved (the substance remaining, but changing in its modifications), this they say is the element and this the principle of things, and therefore they think nothing is either generated or destroyed, since this sort of entity is always conserved . . .*
>
> *Thales, the founder of this type of philosophy, says the principle is water . . . Anaximenes and Diogenes make air prior to water, and the most primary of the simple*

bodies, while Hippasus of Metapontium and Heraclitus of Ephesus say this of fire. (Meta. 983b6–984a6)

The first philosophers asked a very good question: "Of what is reality made?" Without realizing it, they were looking for the *material cause,* but without taking into account the dynamism and the permanence of the existence of all things. In the interests of progress, let us try a different question, says Aristotle. Let us ask ourselves, "Where does reality come from?"

> . . . *e.g. neither the wood nor the bronze causes the change of either of them, nor does the wood manufacture a bed and the bronze a statue, but something else is the cause of the change. And to seek this is to seek the second cause, as we should say — that from which comes the beginning of the movement.* (Meta. 984a24–27)

This other principle is the *efficient cause,* which is easy to identify in the case of manufactured things — it is the joiner who makes the bed. It is more difficult to determine the answer in the case of natural realities. What is the source of movement in nature?

Let us take another question: "What gives things their form?" What is the cause of their particular inner organization, their interior architecture? What gives them their shape and style? Or rather, what determines that a thing is such a thing, that a man is a man? To seek the *formal cause* is to ask ourselves questions about what defines a thing, what makes it recognizable. When confronted with a drinking glass, there is no mistaking it. Its form tells us that it is a drinking glass.

Aristotle, however, wishes to break away from Plato's concept of a prototype. What he is interested in is that which exists concretely — in its concrete form; it is that donkey I can see grazing in the grass and not the prototype of a donkey. But how are we to define the form of a donkey? The formal cause is one of the most difficult to identify, especially in nature.

Aristotle's criticism of Platonic ideas is precisely that they give no explanation of the movement, the transition from possibility to actuality. Plato becomes entrenched in the formal cause. But the genesis of beings has somehow to be explained. The efficient cause can only be explained by the final cause, and not by chance, as some pre-Socratic philosophers seem to suggest.

> . . . *nor again could it be right to entrust so great a matter* [the universe] *to spontaneity and chance.* (Meta. 984b12)

The last question about things is the one that best reveals their reason for being: "Why was this thing made? With a view to what?" This is the *final cause*, the most interesting and the one that we discover last.

> *That for whose sake actions and changes and move-ments take place, they assert to be a cause in a way, but not in this way, i.e. not in the way in which it is its nature to be a cause. For those who speak of reason or friendship class these causes as goods; they do not speak, however, as if anything that exists either existed or came into being for the sake of these, but as if movements started from these. In the same way those* [Plato?] *who say*

the One or the existent is the good, say that it is the cause of substance, but not that substance either is or comes to be for the sake of this. Therefore it turns out that in a sense they both say and do not say the good is a cause; for they do not call it a cause qua *good but only incidentally.* (Meta. 988b6–15)

The material cause, the efficient cause, the formal cause, and the final cause. By increasing the number of questions and lines of approach, Aristotle extricates his thinking from its impasse. Things have definition and at the same time are in a state of movement towards an end, an objective. These four causes are a way of knowing a thing, and the final cause has more explanatory value than the others. Aristotle refers to it as the cause of causes. It is the one that provides the best explanation, because it reveals the "why." It ranks as the *primary cause.*

. . . men do not think they know a thing till they have grasped the "why" of it (which is to grasp the primary cause). (Phys. 194b19)

Knowledge, according to Aristotle, requires patience. How penetrating a gaze do we need in order to grasp the "why" of things? In the case of the man in the street, I could just ask, "Why are you doing that?" But when it comes to natural realities, it is not quite so simple. And yet the final cause is the keystone of knowledge.

The Ultimate Final Cause
What kind of vision is Aristotle ultimately seeking? First he seeks to broaden his perspective, to extend it beyond

familiar things, towards the highest, most divine realities. Nature has an extraordinary abundance of things to offer that are passionately interesting to study. There is also the sky with its heavenly bodies, the movement of which has something divine about it. Aristotle never limits his inquiry to man; there are things nobler than him. It is as if man were borne along by the universe. Man is mortal, and the stars and the universe are eternal.

> . . . *it would be strange to think that the art of politics, or practical wisdom, is the best knowledge, since man is not the best thing in the world.* (NE 1141a20–22)

> . . . *for there are other things much more divine in their nature even than man, e.g. most conspicuously, the bodies of which the heavens are framed.* (NE 1141b1)

The ancient Greeks had not reached the level of knowledge of our astrophysicists, but they were fascinated by the motion of the heavenly bodies, by their very regular movement, which seemed inalterable: a simple movement — displacement about the sky — that seemed to escape the cycle of "generation and corruption" of realities here below. All these things made them think the heavenly bodies were among the eternal realities. Man, too, is endowed with movement, not only with locomotion, but with all forms of "becoming": growth, intellectual progress, but also corruption and death. The stars are simpler in the manner in which they move; they seem incorruptible, immortal. What is more, they constitute the world, in that, without the stars, the sky would collapse, whereas man can pass away without affecting the world. All this makes Aristotle think that the stars are the highest and most divine realities among visible things.

Through the practice of contemplating the stars, the intelligence learns to see further. It progresses in contemplation.

The intelligence must also learn to see each thing in its deepest dimension, which is to say from the point of view of its end. Where is it going? What is its good? These are the questions that the intelligence must ask if it wishes to grasp a thing at its source. Aristotle thinks the human mind is capable of this; he must himself have undergone a very powerful intellectual experience of the source of being. He came to the understanding that the source of everything is the good towards which it tends, and that consequently true knowledge sees things from the point of view of their end. The evolution of a flower is understood in relation to the end at which it aims: the bearing of fruit. But things are not isolated. There is an order in the universe that holds everything together. In the end the flower returns to the earth, because everything is in a state of movement, and that is another good. To learn to contemplate is thus also to get used to seeing things as part of a whole, to see that all things tend towards their good, but also co-operate ultimately in one final good.

God and the Gods for the Greeks and Aristotle

In Aristotle's day, Greek civilization was steeped in religiosity, and all thinkers and men of goodwill referred to the divine. The origins of the Greek religion lay in myth, liturgy, and religious sacrifice, but also in mystery. A.-J. Festugière's book *L'Idéal religieux des Grecs et l'Évangile*[3] describes how for the Greeks, the human world was surrounded by gods who alone were blessed, eternal, and endowed with immortality, gods that people dreamed of resembling:

If only one could be a god! Happiness, eternal happiness, was the privilege of divinity. If one could only therefore become like a divinity, belong to his family, join the race of the gods. If only the abyss that separated the two races could be spanned, and there could be a different relationship between them from that of slave and master, or citizen and the god of a city, or sick person and healer, if there could be a more complete union that affected the very nature of man and, by showing him to have a kinship with the divine, gave him the right, after death, to enter the company of the gods!

Was this a dream? Was it just a dream? Or was it not rather a question of attaining that which was most human in man, that which was most essential and specific to his nature? In such a way that only those who achieved this apotheosis were truly men, and only those wise men who were godlike were truly wise.

This was the aspiration of Greek thought. It was Plato who first gave it specific formulation. And the link he established between the concepts of being, the divine and immortality, were to leave their imprint on subsequent theological speculation.

The feeling that motivated him grafted itself on popular belief. Essentially, this blessed immortality desired by men was only to be achieved by a process of becoming divine. In order to become immortal, one had to be made a god. For immortality, in the fullest sense of the word, was strictly a divine privilege. Immortality did

*not belong in any way to man, in his capacity as such.
He had begun to be and must end. Birth called for
death. Man could only therefore become immortal by
changing his condition, his nature. More precisely,
according to Plato, by allowing his true nature to find
fulfillment; or, through the mysteries,[4] creating a closer
link between oneself and a god.*

Aristotle lived in a culture steeped in this notion of the
gods. As a philosopher he wants to pursue the divine,
which alone enables man to extricate himself from a world
in which everything is "becoming" and birth leads inevitably
to death. He believes, however, that religion has been fal-
sified over the ages.

*Our forefathers in the most remote ages have handed
down to their posterity a tradition in the form of a myth,
that these bodies are gods and that the divine encloses the
whole of nature. The rest of the tradition has been added
later in mythical form with a view to the persuasion of
the multitude and to its legal and utilitarian expediency;
they say these gods are in the form of men. . . . But if one
were to separate the first point from these additions and
take it alone — that they thought the first substances to
be gods, one must regard this as an inspired utterance,
and reflect that, while probably each art and each science
has often been developed as far as possible and has again
perished, these opinions, with others, have been preserved
until the present like relics of the ancient treasure. Only
thus far, then, is the opinion of our ancestors and of our
earliest predecessors clear to us.* (Meta. 1074b1–14)

Aristotle recognized the heroic virtue of Socrates,[6] who claimed to be "serving God" and who placed this service above all else, above his own reputation and life: "Athenians, I love you, but I would rather obey God than you"; "I would never do otherwise [than what was asked by God] if I had to die a thousand times over." In the presence of his judges, Socrates explained the true rule of conduct which was also his: Any man who had chosen a position because he judged it to be the most honourable, or who had been placed there by a superior, must remain there, no matter what the danger, and not think of death, nor any other peril but above all of the shame. It would be a grave offence "to desert a position to which — I believe and am convinced — God called me, ordaining that I should live as a philosopher, examining myself and others." The great offence, as far as Socrates is concerned, is "disobeying one better than oneself, be he God or man."

As for Aristotle, he affirms the importance of religion in society:

> . . . *people who are puzzled to know whether one ought to honour the gods . . . need punishment.* (Top. 105a5)

> *We must see how many things are indispensable to the existence of a state. . . . First, there must be food; secondly, arts, for life requires many instruments; thirdly, there must be arms, for the members of a community have need of them, and in their own hands, too, in order to maintain authority both against disobedient subjects and against external assailants; fourthly there must be a certain amount of revenue, both for internal needs, and for the purposes of*

war; fifthly, or rather first, there must be a care of religion, which is commonly called worship. (Pol. 1328b3–11)

Religion is essentially doing what is right with respect to "the gods, whom it is our duty to honour," that is to say, worship and devotion. It can also prepare our hearts and minds for a virtuous life and channel our affectivity so that we live well.

But what is this religion? Is it monotheistic or polytheistic? Aristotle seems to be saying that the true tradition has been perverted: "They say these gods are in the form of men or like some of the other animals." So religion has been turned into acts of piety motivated by fear or gain. Faithful to his method of being attentive to human reality and all that is human, Aristotle gives value to religion. It can help men to live humanly and become virtuous, and to recognize that above them there is the divine, which must be honoured. He wishes, however, to purge religion of everything that is illusion. For him, metaphysics, far from suppressing religion, gives it a foundation and certainties that it otherwise risks losing with the passage of time.

The Object of Metaphysics

The question arises, then, as to what human intelligence can tell us about God. Therein lies the whole thrust of philosophy and, more specifically, metaphysics.

Aristotle wants truth. He wants to establish a science of truth. Make no mistake; metaphysics is in some respects a very difficult science. We should not take lightly or over-simplify the means by which Aristotle comes to an intellectual knowledge of God. It is not an easy process of deduction. We need a level of intelligence that goes beyond the mere establishment of facts or an investigation of the *how*. Metaphysics seeks to go beyond any notions of such-and-such a thing or such-and-such a group of things, to grasp the very being of things. That is why Aristotle says that the object of metaphysical study is being *in virtue of its own nature* and not in its capacity as such-and-such a thing.

To be convinced of the rigour of Aristotelian thought, we have only to read the *Metaphysics*, his analysis of substance, actuality, and potency, of the "one" and the "many," of motion, and of the definition of words in Book 5. Aristotle seeks to penetrate the being of visible things and their movement, from their generation to their decay. He hopes to come to know the light residing in them, their intelligibility, their capacity to be grasped by human intelligence. And so he looks at their being, their existence, but he also recognizes that visible things do not possess their existence; they are things in a state of motion, of "becoming." From the way they come to be and yet do not have fullness of being in themselves, Aristotle deduces that beyond them there must necessarily be a being that simply *is*, eternally. Aristotelian contemplation is the penetrating gaze of reason that sees — not with the eyes, but with the intelligence — a presence, the god.

How does the metaphysician see God? On the basis of the reality of movement and becoming, Aristotle seeks the origin of becoming, for all movement implies not only an efficient cause, a mover, but above all a reason for the existence of the movement, a good that gives rise to the movement, which is the final cause.

There is therefore also something which moves it [the First Heaven, which is the source of movement in the universe] *and since that which is moved and moves is intermediate, there is something which moves without being moved, being eternal, substance and actuality. And the object of desire and the object of thought move in this way; they move without being moved.* (Meta. 1072a21)

Aristotle also notes, "If it were not true, the world would have proceeded out of night and 'all things together' (universal confusion) and out of non-being" (Meta. 1072a19–20), a possibility that he considers absurd. It would be a negation of the intelligence.

The first mover, then, exists of necessity; and in so far as it exists by necessity, its mode of being is good, and it is in this sense the first principle. . . . On such a principle, then, depend the heavens and the world of nature. (Meta. 1072b10–14)

In some very dense texts (Meta. 1072b14–21), Aristotle tries to grasp what this life of God and in God is. God is the sovereign thought that thinks on itself, for in God "the intelligence and the intelligible are the same." And Aristotle adds that God always has the immense joy of contemplation — the joy that we possess only for a few fleeting moments.

We say therefore that God is a living being, eternal, most [the supreme] *good, so that life and duration continuous and eternal belong to God; for this is God.* (Meta. 1072b26–30)

Finally, Aristotle asks himself in what way the universe contains the good, the sovereign good:

> ... *whether as something separate and by itself, or as the order of the parts. Probably in both ways, as an army does; for its good is found both in its order and in its leader, and more in the latter; for he does not depend on the order but it depends on him. And all things are ordered together somehow, but not all alike — both fishes and fowls and plants; and the world is not such that one thing has nothing to do with another, but they are connected. For all are ordered together to one end.* (Meta. 1075a11–18)

Obviously, the wiser the philosopher becomes, the more this capacity to philosophize and contemplate takes root in him, the more this activity of looking at God, in and through visible things and their movement, becomes a source of joy. It becomes the happiest, most blessed, most joyous activity and the source of immense — I dare even say ecstatic — pleasure. This activity is not then intellectual investigation, a laborious labour, but *leisure*. It is as if the intelligence has finally attained its principal object. It rests in this object. Of course the word "leisure" does not mean here what we commonly use it to mean, the opposite of serious activity. It is the perfection of intellectual activity, which pauses and marvels in the greatest and finest of its objects: God. Thus the wise man extricates himself from the law of becoming and movement, from that of stress and political activity, to attain the eternal: the prime, unmoved mover. Through contemplation, he takes his place, for a brief moment, outside time.

And happiness is thought to depend on leisure; for we are busy that we may have leisure, and make war that we may live in peace. (NE 1177b4–5)

So if among virtuous actions, political and military actions are distinguished by nobility and greatness, and these are unleisurely and aim at an end and are not desirable for their own sake, but the activity of reason, which is contemplative, seems both to be superior in serious worth and to aim at no end beyond itself, and to have its pleasure proper to itself (and this augments the activity), and the self sufficiency, leisureliness, unweariedness (so far as this is possible for man), and all the other attributes ascribed to the supremely happy man are evidently those connected with this activity, it follows that this will be the complete happiness of man, if it be allowed a complete term of life (for none of the attributes of happiness is incomplete). (NE 1177b15–25)

. . . for what we do to the gods and the most godlike of men is to call them blessed and happy. (NE 1101b24)

But such a life [that of contemplation] *would be too high for man; for it is not in so far as he is man that he will live so, but in so far as something divine is present in him; and by so much as this is superior to our composite nature is its activity superior to that which is the exercise of the other kind of virtue. If reason is divine, then, in comparison with man, the life according to it is divine in comparison with human life. But we must not follow*

those who advise us, being men, to think of human things,
and, being mortal, of mortal things, but must, so far as
we can, make ourselves immortal, and strain every nerve
to live in accordance with the best thing in us; for even if
it be small in bulk, much more does it in power and
worth surpass everything. (NE 1177b26–1178a2)

Even though, on the metaphysical plane, Aristotle, after meticulous investigation, asserts that the prime, unmoved mover is the source of all movement in the universe and that the whole universe is thus ordered by it, in the same way that a general determines the order of his army, he does not state explicitly that God watches over mankind. Steeped in the Greek culture as he was and respectful of human laws and ancient truths handed down from earlier times, Aristotle, basing his thought on general opinion and that of wise men, nevertheless affirms on many occasions in his works that the gods do have a care for human affairs (NE 1179a24). They know everything (Poet. 1454b5, Rhet. 1397b12), they introduce order into the universe (Pol. 1326a32), they give men gifts (NE 1099b12), and they come to the rescue of victims of injustice, the wronged (Rhet. 1383b9). He tells us that Homer was right to call Zeus "father of gods and men," because he was the king of them all (Pol. 1259b13). Aristotle tells us that God recognizes our offerings and that good fortune depends upon him (EE 1243b12, 1248b).

Metaphysical contemplation is an act of the intelligence. It is like the accomplishment of that which is most marvellous in a human being and the universe. At the same time, however, it is an activity that honours God.

This is what R. A. Gauthier tells us in his commentary on the *Nichomachean Ethics*: "What disappeared with Aristotle was probably the idea of a god that was not entirely intelligible and of a knowledge that was not entirely that of the intelligence. But for all its intellectual nature, Aristotelian contemplation, even in the *Ethics*, remains, if not mystical, at least religious. It does not separate contemplation from honouring, because it knows that in contemplating it does not touch the smallest part of God, and that it must adore the immensity of that which, in the one whom it loves, eludes it."[7]

Philosophical Contemplation and Mystical Experience
At times Plato's dialogues give the impression of an actual experience of God. We have only to read the *Symposium* or the *Phaedo* to be convinced. In Plato, poetry is intermingled with mysticism. Aristotle wishes to root his knowledge of God in a proper philosophical science. In his philosophy there is no room for myth, illusion, or poetry. He does acknowledge, however, in his first ethical treatise, the *Eudemian Ethics*, that there are such things as inspired people or prophets.

> . . . *those are called fortunate who, whatever they start on, succeed in it without being good at reasoning. And deliberation is of no advantage to them, for they have in them a principle that is better than intellect and deliberation, while the others have not this but have intellect; they have inspiration but they cannot deliberate. For, though lacking reason, they succeed.* (EE 1248a30 – 33)[8]

It would seem that we are to see these inspired people more as men who possess a divine instinct higher than virtue, than as the poets of whom Plato speaks, prophets and fortune-tellers.

Aristotelian contemplation is not then an experience of or an encounter with God, as in Christian mysticism. Nor is it an ascetic life designed to produce a void or to get in touch with the real self, as in certain Eastern religions. It is allied to aesthetic contemplation in which man is at leisure as he looks with wonder upon the beauty through which the divine beauty is radiated.

Contemplation as a Blessed Moment that Gives Meaning to a Lifetime

The wise man who has caught a glimpse of God through visible things is thus a fully accomplished man. Such an experience, if it is nourished and reproduced, will give a new perspective to all life and all human activities. The wise man is no longer embroiled in the quarrels and conflicts of state. He stands back from them. He sees things from a standpoint of humility born of the fact that he recognizes himself to be subject to truth and the pursuit of it. By looking in the direction of God, the Eternal, he sees himself to be small and finite, even though he bears within him a treasure: the capacity to know.

Certainly Aristotle is aware that few people will have the leisure to lead this divine, almost superhuman, life. But he seeks to show that only those who do will be able to experience complete happiness in accordance with the deepest aspirations of human beings. Others will be happy insofar as they are able and according to their possibilities (as we shall see in the following chapters), but they will not experience the greatest happiness of all. Aristotle, a philosopher who knows that most people follow their passions, will show that only those who devote themselves to wisdom and at the same time live out their humanity with friends and family and within the context of the state, will know the most complete happiness. Is that not why, in his *Politics*, he wants the legislators to encourage citizens to progress in that direction? It matters not how many attain true happiness; what matters is that those who desire it are able to orient themselves towards the knowledge that is the greatest and the noblest for man.

Having seen how Aristotle describes wisdom, may we not attribute to him, by analogy, what the Greek-speaking Jews of a later period said of wisdom?

> *I esteemed her more than sceptres and thrones;*
> *Compared with her, I held riches as nothing, I reckoned no priceless*
> *Stone to be her peer, for compared with her, all gold is a pinch of*
> *Sand, and beside her silver ranks as mud.*
> *I loved her more than health or beauty,*
> *Preferred her to the light,*
> *Since her radiance never sleeps.*
> — Wisdom 7, 8–14[8]

CHAPTER 4

VIRTUES GREAT AND SMALL

In the previous chapter we tried to see with Aristotle what we can hope to discover through our desire and our capacity to know the truth about the world. In Aristotle's estimation, this desire is not fruitless. We can come to know the final causes. The intelligence then pauses, wonders, and contemplates.

For Aristotle, the philosopher or wise man is the one who attains true human happiness. But we must be careful! Even if he appears to be the most divine of men, the wise man is still a man, subject to fatigue, illness, and death. He needs a family. He needs friends to journey with him to the point of contemplation.

Just like any other man, the wise man has had to work on everything within him that makes up his humanity: his passions, his propensity to anger, his sense of pleasure, his relationships with others. How could he be happy if he were like a chameleon, inconstant in his friendships, or if he were afraid of a fly? In order to be a fully accomplished human being, a happy man, he must be master of himself, with an inner structure. Today we might say that a man or woman needs to be upstanding, honest, and true, clear about his or her choices. This structure or inner stability arises from what Aristotle calls the "virtues." We have talked about wisdom being the supreme virtue. Not everyone, however, can devote himself to philosophy and the pursuit of knowledge of what is most noble. Others may find their happiness in the practice of moral virtues, aimed at the good of others in society.

It is for this reason that, in line with other Greek philosophers and moralists, Aristotle devotes several chapters to the different virtues and vices — that is to say, to the way in which we manage our desires and passions, in which we control them or allow them to control us. This catalogue of virtues and vices contains a detailed analysis of human psychology. It shows how the desirous part — the passions — is often motivated by fear or by an exorbitant need to *appear*, to possess and to experience pleasure.

When a man lets himself go, he has a tendency to become fossilized in an attitude of excess or deficiency, and sometimes to go from one extreme to another. He gorges himself and then fasts to regain his health, or he may habitually stray into an excess of food or drink, even drugs. By contrast, the man who possesses the virtue of temperance enjoys eating and drinking without excess. He knows how to take pleasure without being overrun by it. He governs himself with rectitude because he knows how to integrate the *logos* in his life.

Virtue is this inner disposition that we acquire through performance and habit, which enable us to regulate our desires or their opposites — our fears — because they have allowed themselves to be penetrated by the *logos*.

In order to understand the virtues, Aristotle compares each one to its opposite. He tells us that virtue is the *mean* between two extremes, between excess as a result of too much and deficiency as a result of too little. But, of course, this happy medium does not reflect quantity; it is the high point or ideal. Diagrammatically this would be represented in the form of a triangle.

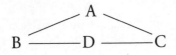

If we take the example of the virtue of courage, B would be its excess: recklessness. C would be its extreme deficit: cowardice. A would be the ideal, the pinnacle: courage attained through struggle and real work on oneself. And D would be the happy medium in the quantitative sense, which is not to be confused with virtue.

Courage and Temperance

Aristotle starts by analyzing those moral virtues that concern man's inner equilibrium, such as courage and temperance, which regulate the passions in relation to oneself. *Courage* is, above all, that quality in a man that enables him to stand firm in face of danger. He differs from both the coward who flees in fear, and from the vainglorious, oblivious adventurer who plunges ahead, sometimes in the hope of acclaim. The brave man knows how to meet with difficulties, even in his flesh. He is aware of the price. He may be afraid, but he stands firm. Honed by reason, his sensibility has been rendered capable of withstanding trials. He stands firm because it is his duty. He stands firm because it is good to act in such a way.

> *Properly, then, he will be called brave who is fearless in face of a noble death, and of all emergencies that involve death; and the emergencies of war are in the highest degree of this kind.* (NE 1115a33–35)

Thus courage reveals itself in extreme situations in which lives are put at risk. The greatest danger is death. For Aristotle, the supremely brave man is the soldier, for whom death in battle is always on the horizon. What are the contemporary forms of courage? In what situations are our lives most exposed? Possibly in certain situations where people stand up to pressure — the pressure of hatred or corruption, the pressure to conform or to be excessively individualistic. Today the brave person may be the one who endures situations of extreme violence yet responds with an attitude that is nonviolent. The virtue of courage is still with us, though the nature of the battle is not necessarily the same.

Temperance is the virtue that regulates bodily pleasures, especially those derived from touch, "in the case of food and in that of drink and in that of sexual intercourse" (NE 1118a30). Touch as the basis of all the senses is also the sensation most sought after by sensualists.

> *That is why a certain gourmand prayed that his throat might become longer than a crane's, implying that it was the contact that he took pleasure in.* (NE 1118a30)

One might think that this gourmand was hungry for the taste, but no. What he wants is to prolong "the contact." The gourmand, or the guzzler, to call him by his proper name, is lacking in temperance. He is self-indulgent.

> *The self-indulgent man, then, craves for all pleasant things or those that are most pleasant, and is led by his appetite to choose these at the cost of everything else.* (NE 1119a1)

It should be noted that Aristotle draws a distinction between the person who allows himself through weakness to be carried away and virtually controlled by pleasure, and the person who is deliberately self-indulgent. "The incontinent man is apt to pursue, not on conviction, bodily pleasures that are excessive and contrary to the right rule, while the self-indulgent man is convinced because he is the sort of man to pursue them." (NE 1151a11)

The opposite vice, which is self-indulgence through a lack of any sense of pleasure, does not really have a name, notes Aristotle, who refers to it as "insensibility."

Liberality (Generosity) and Magnificence

The "liberal" man (*éleutherios*) is likely to be a freeman as opposed to a slave. He is a cultivated man who has received a good education and who therefore seeks pleasures suited to that education. He knows how to make use of his leisure. In a more restrained sense, he is a *generous* man. Generosity and magnificence are the virtues that regulate the use of material wealth.

The generous man is the one who gives away his material goods without hesitation and who, by virtue of this fact, will be loved and approved of. He gives as he should, to those he should, when he should, and he does it gladly.

> *It is highly characteristic of a liberal man also to go to excess in giving, so that he leaves too little for himself; for it is the nature of a liberal man not to look to himself. . . Liberality resides not in the multitude of the gifts but in the state of character of the giver, and this is relative to the giver's substance. There is nothing to prevent the man who gives less from being the more liberal man, if he has less to give.* (NE 1120b4–10)

Generosity is a matter of virtue but also of other considerations associated with the circumstances of each individual, notes Aristotle.

> *Those are thought to be more liberal who have not made their wealth but inherited it; for in the first place they have no experience of want, and secondly all men are fonder of their own productions, as are parents and poets.*
>
> *It is not easy for the liberal man to be rich, since he is not apt either at taking or at keeping, but at giving away, and does not value wealth for its own sake but as a means to giving. Hence comes the charge that is brought against fortune, that those who deserve riches most get it least. But it is not unreasonable that it should turn out so; for he cannot have wealth, any more than anything else, if he does not take pains to have it.* (NE 1120b10–19)

One of the vices opposed to generosity is *prodigality*, which is like generosity, but the prodigal man gives excessively to the wrong people and in a way that he should not. He allows himself to be governed by his passion for giving, or rather, by his passion for being surrounded by flattering friends and appearing important.

This is why he is thought to have not a bad character; it is not the mark of a wicked or ignoble man to go to excess in giving and not taking, but only of a foolish one. (NE 1121a26)

But most prodigal people, as has been said, also take from the wrong sources, and are in this respect mean. They become apt to take because they wish to spend and cannot do this easily; for their possessions soon run short. Thus they are forced to provide means from some other source. At the same time, because they care nothing for honour, they take recklessly and from any source; for they have an appetite for giving, and they do not mind how or from what source. Hence also their giving is not liberal; for it is not noble [right], *nor does it aim at nobility* [what is right], *nor is it done in the right way; sometimes they make rich those who should be poor, and will give nothing to people of respectable character, and much to flatterers or those who provide them with some other pleasure.* (NE 1121a30b7)

It is interesting to find Aristotle telling us that there is a form of self-indulgence that arises from excessive giving, a kind of intemperate and misplaced generosity, the purpose of which is to acquire numerous friends and appear important. We immediately think of *meanness* as the opposite of generosity. But giving too much, *when we should not*, can also be harmful. It can be a way of binding our beneficiaries to us, of ensuring that they remain dependent on us rather than enabling them to grow, for example, when we give a man a fish instead of teaching him to fish. The right gift is one that is given to whom it should and when it should, Aristotle says, because the other person needs it, and not in order to rid myself of my compulsion to "appear."

This said, meanness is a real defect of virtue, and is more readily shared — if we can say such a thing — among men than its opposite, prodigality.

> *But meanness is . . . more innate in men than prodigality: for most men are fonder of getting money than giving.* (NE 1121b14)

This is why, with help, it is easier for a prodigal man to become generous than for a mean man. The mean man is self-interested; he wants to possess, to amass. He takes pleasure in his possessions. Because he is closed in on himself, it is more difficult to cure him.

Another virtue, *magnificence*, is concerned with the regulation of giving. The magnificent man is similar to the generous man, except that magnificence relates to honourable and excellent things, whereas generosity relates to lesser things, "and in these it surpasses liberality in scale" (NE 1122a22).

> *Magnificence is an attribute of expenditures of the kind which we call honourable, e.g. those connected with the gods — votive offerings, buildings, and sacrifices — and similarly with any form of religious worship, and all*

116

those that are proper objects of public-spirited ambition, as when people think they ought to equip a chorus or a trireme, or entertain the city, in a brilliant way. (NE 1122b18–23)

Of private occasions of expenditure the most suitable are those that take place once for all, e.g. a wedding or anything of the kind, or anything that interests the whole city or the people of position in it, and also the receiving of foreign guests and the sending of them on their way, and gifts and counter-gifts; for the magnificent man spends not on himself but on public objects, and gifts bear some resemblance to votive offerings. A magnificent man will also furnish his house suitably to his wealth (for even a house is a sort of public ornament), and will spend by preference on those works that are lasting (for these are the most beautiful). (NE 1122b36–1123a10)

The opposite vices are *ostentation* and *parsimony*. The individual who sins by excess, through ostentation, spends beyond what is right:

... on small objects of expenditure he spends much and displays a tasteless showiness; e.g. he gives a club dinner on the scale of a wedding banquet, and when he provides the chorus for a comedy he brings them onto the stage in purple, as they do at Megara. And all such things he will do not for honour's sake but to show off his wealth, and because he thinks he is admired for these things, and where he ought to spend much he spends little and where little, much. (NE 1123a21–27)

As for the stingy man, he will always fall short of what he should spend:

> *. . . he will hesitate and consider how he may spend least, and lament even that, and think he is doing everything on a bigger scale than he ought.* (NE 1123a30)

Good Temper, Amiability, Veracity, and Sense of Humour

Aristotle is also interested in virtues that seem less important but which are nevertheless at the very heart of life, the small virtues that reveal our inner equilibrium, or lack of it, in our relationships with others in society. They include the good temper or aggression we exhibit in our relations, our amiability, the veracity we expect of ourselves in our words and actions, and the sense of humour that colours our social interaction. Such attitudes may seem unimportant, but they say much about the climate of our everyday relations with our fellow-citizens. Because they involve our social relationships, they are closely linked to friendship.

Like courage, *good temper* is a virtue that regulates anger, irascibility or the lack of anger, fear. But courage uses the force of irascibility, to rise to the assault, whereas good temper moderates any irascibility that has been provoked. The good-tempered person is not weak or feeble. He can get angry when necessary. But he also has the secret strength of patience. He stands his ground calmly. Was it not the virtue of nonviolence that Mahatma Gandhi spoke of when he said that, in order to be nonviolent, one had to know how to be violent? By contrast,

> *. . . those who are not angry at the things they should*

be angry at are thought to be fools, and so are those who are not angry in the right way, at the right time, or with the right persons; for such a man is thought not to feel things nor to be pained by them, and, since he does not get angry, he is thought unlikely to defend himself; and to endure being insulted and put up with insult to one's friends is slavish. (NE 1126a3–8)

From another perspective, Aristotle differentiates among choleric people, between those who are hot-tempered and express their anger, and those who do not show their anger initially but allow it to fester within them. The former are irascible; the latter rancorous.

Now hot-tempered people get angry quickly and with the wrong persons and at the wrong things and more than is right, but their anger ceases quickly — which is the best point about them. This happens to them because they do not restrain their anger but retaliate openly owing to their quickness of temper, and then their anger ceases. (NE 1126a14–17)

Sulky people are hard to appease, and retain their anger long; for they repress their passion. But it ceases when they retaliate; for revenge relieves them of their anger, producing in them pleasure instead of pain. If this does not happen they retain their burden; for owing to its not being obvious, no one ever reasons with them, and to digest one's anger in oneself takes time. Such people are most troublesome to themselves and to their dearest friends. (NE 1126a20–28)

Amiability is the middle state between flattery and contrariety.

> *In gatherings of men, in social life and the interchange of words and deeds, some men are thought to be obsequious, viz. those who to give pleasure praise everything and never oppose, but think it their duty "to give no pain to the people they meet"; while those who, on the contrary, oppose everything and care not a whit about giving pain are called churlish and contentious. That the states we have named are culpable is plain enough, and that the middle state is laudable — that in virtue of which a man will put up with, and will resent, the right things and in the right way; but no name has been assigned to it, though it most resembles friendship. For the man who corresponds to this middle state is very much what, with affection added, we call a good friend. But the state in question differs from friendship in that it implies no passion or affection for one's associates; since it is not by reason of loving or hating that such a man takes everything in the right way, but by being a man of a certain kind. For he will behave so alike towards those he knows, and those he does not know, towards intimates and those who are not so, except that in each of these cases he will behave as is befitting; for it is not proper to have the same care for intimates and for strangers, nor again is it the same conditions that make it right to give pain to them. Now we have said generally that he will associate with people in the right way; but it is by reference to what is honourable and expedient that he will aim at not giving pain or at contributing pleasure.* (NE 1126b11–30)

Veracity concerns the image of ourselves that we wish to project to others.

> *... let us now describe those who pursue truth or falsehood alike in words and deeds and in the claims they put forward. The boastful man, then, is thought to be apt to claim the things that bring glory, when he has not got them ... and the mock-modest man on the other hand to disclaim what he has or belittle it, while the man who observes the mean is one who calls a thing by its own name, being truthful both in life and in word, owning to what he has, and neither more nor less.* (NE 1127a18–26)

> *For the man who loves truth, and is truthful where nothing is at stake, will still more be truthful where something is at stake; he will avoid falsehood as something base. ... He inclines rather to understate the truth; for this seems in better taste because exaggerations are wearisome.* (NE 1127b4–7)

After defining the right attitude to adopt when it comes to assessing our own qualities (the way in which we take compliments, for instance), Aristotle evokes the two attitudes that are not balanced: *boastfulness* and *reticence*. They may both be forms of falsehood.

> *He who claims more than he has with no ulterior object* [reputation or gain, for example] *is a contemptible sort of fellow (otherwise he would not have delighted in falsehood), but seems futile rather than bad; but if he does it for an object, he who does it for the sake of reputation or honour is (for a boaster) not*

very much to be blamed, but he who does it for money, or the things that lead to money, is an uglier character. (NE 1127b10–14)

Mock-modest people, who understate things, seem more attractive in character; for they are thought to speak not for gain but to avoid parade; and here too it is qualities which bring reputation that they disclaim. . . . Those who disclaim trifling and obvious qualities are called humbugs and are more contemptible; and sometimes this seems to be boastfulness. (NE 1127b23–28)

Aristotle is also interested in the way in which a man relaxes with others: Is he playful or the opposite, grumpy? Does he carry humour to excess like a clown? Isn't relaxation another form of rest, a different form of leisure from that of contemplation, but nonetheless one on which virtue has a bearing because it is a state that is eminently human?

Since life includes rest as well as activity, and in this is included leisure and amusement, there seems here to be a kind of intercourse which is tasteful; there is such a thing as saying — and again listening to — what one should and as one should. The kind of people one is speaking or listening to will also make a difference. . . . Those who carry humour to excess are thought to be vulgar buffoons, striving after humour at all costs, and aiming rather at raising a laugh than at saying what is becoming and avoiding pain to the object of their fun; while those who can neither make a joke themselves nor put up

*with those who do are thought to be boorish and unpol-
ished. But those who joke in a tasteful way are called
ready-witted.* (NE 1127b37–1128a11)

Magnanimity: The Accomplishment of Humanity

The man who has integrated all the virtues — courage,
temperance, amiability, generosity — is really at the peak
of moral happiness, that is to say, happiness plain and
simple. He is the happiest of men because his humanity is
truly accomplished and radiant. This blossoming of a
human being who has integrated all the virtues so that they
have become inner and almost natural dispositions Aristotle calls *magnanimity.*[1]

Aristotle does not spend much time describing the two
extremes of which this virtue is the middle state. The vain
man who thinks himself worthy of great honour is in reality the fool who does not know himself. He seeks to make
himself out to be important, he wears splendid clothes but
is empty inside, and everyone sees what he really is (NE
1125a27–32). *Pusillanimity,* on the other hand, is a more
widespread and worse vice. The pusillanimous man is
capable but does not dare to act. He lacks confidence in
himself and is overrun with fear.

Magnanimity is not to be seen as a supplementary
virtue, but one that recapitulates all the others and reveals
them all to the maximum. It "seems to be a sort of crown
of the virtues; for it makes them greater, and it is not found
without them" (NE 1124a1–3).

The magnanimous man is the most autonomous. He
has no need of others. He is not worried about what others

may think of him. It is as if he were above all that. His great concern is the good, moral perfection, he knows how valuable it is. Because he is capable of great things, he expects recognition and honours, but he is truly worthy of them. Thus the magnanimous man is the perfect man.

Now the proud [magnanimous] *man, since he deserves most, must be good in the highest degree.* (NE 1123b27)

Aristotle enjoyed describing this magnanimous man. Was this, in his view, a more or less attainable ideal? Did he have a particular model in mind? In any case, for him, this is a great man, a capable man who does not demean himself with petty concerns. He is a little like a god, superior to ordinary mortals. It is possible that history has produced such men.

He does not run into trifling dangers, nor is he fond of danger, because he honours few things; but he will face great dangers, and when he is in danger he is unsparing of his life, knowing that there are conditions on which life is not worth having. And he is the sort of man to confer benefits but he is ashamed of receiving them; for the one is the mark of a superior, the other of an inferior. (NE 1124b7–12)

It is a mark of the proud man also to ask for nothing or scarcely anything, but to give help readily, and to be dignified towards people who enjoy high position and good fortune, but unassuming towards those of the middle class; for it is a difficult and lofty thing to be superior to the former, but easy to be so to the latter, and a lofty bearing over the former is no mark of ill-breeding, but among humble people it is as vulgar as a display of strength against the weak.

Again it is a characteristic of the proud man not to aim at the things commonly held in honour, or the things in which others excel; to be sluggish and to hold back except where great honour or a great work is at stake, and to be a man of few deeds, but of great and notable ones (NE 1124b19–25)

He must also be open in his hate and in his love (for to conceal one's feelings, i.e. to care less for truth than for what people will think, is a coward's part), and must speak and act openly; for he is free of speech because he is contemptuous, and he is given to telling the truth, except when he speaks in irony to the vulgar. He must be unable to make his life revolve round another, unless it be a friend; for this is slavish. . . . Nor is he given to admiration; for nothing to him is great. Nor is he mindful of wrongs; for it is not the part of a proud man to have a long memory, especially for wrongs, but rather to overlook them. Nor is he a gossip; for he will speak neither about himself nor about another, since he cares not to be praised nor for others to be blamed; nor again is he given to praise; and for the same reason he is not an evil-speaker, even about his enemies, except from haughtiness.

With regard to necessary or small matters he is least of all men given to lamentation or the asking of favours; for it is the part of one who takes such matters seriously to behave so with respect to them. He is one who will possess beautiful and profitless things rather than profitable and useful ones; for this is more proper to a character that suffices to itself. (NE 1124b27–1125a13)

Such a man does not pass unnoticed. He is recognizable by his physical bearing!

Further a slow step is thought proper to the proud man, a deep voice, and a level utterance; for the man who takes few things seriously is not likely to be hurried, nor the man who thinks nothing great to be excited. (NE 1125a13–14)

At first glance, this magnanimous man might be taken to be a very proud man in the modern sense of the word. He seeks to be perfectly accomplished. Is he not, underneath it all, seeking his own aggrandizement and perfection? We shall see a little further on that this is not in fact the case. The proud man (in the conventional modern sense) is the centre of his own world. He is not interested in others. Whereas, for Aristotle, the magnanimous man is interested in others, and in a manner that is great and noble.

The Virtue of Justice

After magnanimity, is there room for any other virtue? There is, if we look at how we relate to others, which also needs rectifying. That is why the last virtue Aristotle considers is that of justice, which does not imply our own perfection or accomplishment alone, but the manner in which we live and work for others in society.

This form of [legal] *justice, then, is complete virtue, but not absolutely, but in relation to our neighbour. And therefore justice is often thought to be the greatest of virtues, and "neither evening nor morning star" is so wonderful; and proverbially "in justice is every virtue comprehended."*

And it is complete virtue in its fullest sense, because it is the actual exercise of complete virtue. It is complete because he who possesses it can exercise his virtue not only in himself but towards his neighbour also; for many men can exercise virtue in their own affairs, but not in their relations to their neighbour. This is why the saying of Bias is thought to be true, that "rule will show the man"; for a ruler is necessarily in relation to other men and a member of a society. For this same reason justice, alone of the virtues, is thought to be "another's good," because it is related to our neighbour; for it does what is advantageous to another, either a ruler or a copartner. Now the worst man is he who exercises his wickedness both towards himself and towards his friends, and the best man is not he who exercises his virtue towards himself but he who exercises it towards another; for this is a difficult task. (NE 1129b26–1130a8)

This virtue that is exercised in relation to others provides the structure for life in the city-state, or ideal political community. In a family, people conduct their relations with others according to a certain unwritten code of justice; this happens of its own accord among those who wish to live happily together. On a wider social scale, our relations with others need to be codified into law. The law is, or should be, an expression of justice, or at very least the expression of a certain respect for others. Thus, in its primary sense, to be just is to observe the law.

> *Since the lawless man was seen to be unjust and the law-abiding man just, evidently all lawful acts are in a sense just acts, for the acts laid down by the legislative art are lawful, and each of these, we say, is just. Now the laws in their enactments on all subjects aim at the common advantage either of all or of the best or of those who hold power, or something of the sort; so that in one sense we call those acts just that tend to produce and preserve happiness and its components for the political society.* (NE 1129b11–18)

Like all the ancient Greeks, Aristotle has a very elevated idea of the law. It should encourage people to be virtuous because the good and respect of others are dependent on its doing so. Thus slander and adultery are infringements of justice, and the law should prevent them.

> *And the law bids us do both the acts of a brave man (e.g. not to desert our post nor take to flight nor throw away our arms), and those of a temperate man (e.g. not to commit adultery nor to gratify one's lust), and those of a good-tempered man (e.g. not to strike another nor to speak evil).* (NE 1129b19–23)

This may well be shocking to those of us who are used to separating the private from the public domain and to legislating in terms of the rights of the individual. With Aristotle, we are dealing with an era well before our modern age and far removed from our individualistic attitudes.

To be a citizen is the function of a freeman. It is a privilege to participate in the life of the city-state. The law should favour life together and, in doing so, encourage virtue. These two facets are inseparable.

Some aspects of the law, however, seem artificial and relative. Why should we drive on the left rather than the right? Our human sciences have studied the customs of different societies in depth, and have shown that there are often huge discrepancies among them. What is just in some is not in others. This is why Aristotle draws a distinction between *natural justice* and *particular justice*. Homicide and theft are always unjust, no matter where they occur. Complying with a traffic light, on the other hand, is a matter for particular justice.

> *Of political justice part is natural, part legal — natural, that which everywhere has the same force and does not exist by people's thinking this or that: legal, that which is originally indifferent, but when it has been laid down is not indifferent, e.g. that a prisoner's ransom shall be a mina, or that a goat and not two sheep shall be sacrificed, and again all the laws that are passed for particular cases, e.g. that sacrifice shall be made in honour of Brasidas, and the provisions of decrees.* (NE 1134b18–24)

And Aristotle notes that some of his predecessors, some Sophists, maintained that what was prescribed by particular law was always contrary to natural law and based on force. To them, injustice was the law of nature, and justice the product of a contract between men. The opposition of nature and the law had become common among the Sophists.

But for Aristotle, as for Plato, natural justice cannot be assimilated with the law of force. There is ambiguity about the word "nature." Nature in Aristotle does not mean a state of spontaneous being, but the profound essence of being. Natural justice should also be understood as that which flows from the deepest aspirations of the *logos*. And because it imposes itself on all those who possess the *logos*, it is universal to humankind. It has the same force everywhere.

This distinction between natural and universal law and particular law is pinpointed in two texts in the *Rhetoric*:

> By the two kinds of law I mean particular law and universal law. Particular law is that which each community lays down and applies to its own members; this is partly written and partly unwritten. Universal law is the law of nature. For there really is, as everyone to some extent divines, a natural justice and injustice that is binding on all men, even on those who have no association or covenant with each other. It is this that Sophocles' Antigone clearly means when she says that the burial of Polynices was a just act in spite of the prohibition: she means that it was just by nature.
>
> > Not of to-day or yesterday it is,
> > But lives eternal: none can date its birth.
> > —Antigone, 456–7
>
> And so Empedocles, when he bids us kill no living creature, says that this is not just for some people while unjust for others,
>
> > Nay, but, an all-embracing law, through the realms of the sky

Unbroken it stretcheth, and over the earth's
immensity . . .

(Rhet. 1373b1–17)

We must urge that the principles of equity are perma-
nent and changeless, and that the universal law does not
change either, for it is the law of nature, whereas written
laws often do change. (Rhet. 1375a30–32)

Natural Justice

Natural justice is thus the basis for legal justice. It is the same everywhere; it is universal. It is the basis for morality. That is why murder, adultery, and theft are always and universally condemned (NE 1107a11).

Aristotle disagrees, then, with the Sophists, who hold that most men follow their passions and seek their own interests, and that this proves that they are by nature unjust. It is only the legal law that obliges them to be just.

The Aristotelian vision is a powerful contradiction to the Sophists: it is optimistic. A human being is made for happiness. This is his deepest inclination. He is endowed with reason and therefore capable, by nature, of controlling himself. Obviously Aristotle recognizes that most men follow their passions; he records as much. But where does this ill come from? Aristotle does not try to answer this question. Rather, he maintains that, with good laws, good dispositions, good education, and good choices, man can achieve happiness, albeit after much struggle.

But what is natural? The way in which Aristotle talks about women being inferior to men and made to obey

(Pol. 1260a12), and of men being made to command, and of the natural slave, shows to what extent Aristotle belonged to the culture of his day. For him a slave is a being incapable of reason and deliberate choice (Pol. 1280a33). He is a kind of intellectually deficient being who is not a complete man. He has been provided by nature to carry out manual work so that other, "free" men may devote themselves to nobler causes. The slave is a living tool, the property of a freeman, a sort of extension of his body (Pol. 1254a9 cont.). Other texts, however, appear to suggest a very different viewpoint. In them Aristotle speaks of the possibility of liberating slaves and giving them their freedom as a reward (Pol. 1330a32). He even left instructions in his will for the liberation of slaves who had been in his service.[2] Elsewhere Aristotle refers to the slave who, as a man (NE 1161b5–8), may be a friend to a freeman, and he presents both slaves and women as beings capable of exercising the virtues of courage, temperance, and justice, though always within the parameters of their particular duties (Pol. 1260a17–b25). At very least, Aristotle is ambiguous on the subject of slaves.

Perhaps he was torn between what he saw as a cultural fact — recognized by everyone — and his personal intuition of the virtue of some slaves. What is certain is that the economy and operation of Greek city-states depended on the existence of slaves. Affirming their full and complete humanity risked upsetting the whole system of the day. Could Aristotle afford to cause that kind of revolution?

If there is ambiguity in the notion of natural and universal law in Aristotle, he did nevertheless lay down a fundamental principle, the same principle evoked by Antigone, that dates back to ancient times. It has resurfaced in our day under another guise, that of the Universal Declaration of Human Rights of 1948. But because of his cultural background, perhaps also because of his desire not to provoke too much political upheaval, Aristotle was not able to affirm that every human being had equal rights.

The Just Man as One Who Voluntarily Obeys the Law
If, then, the just man is the one who observes the *correctly established* law, the virtue of justice — like its opposite, the vice of injustice — implies that he acts voluntarily. Aristotle identifies three different kinds of injury or moral wrong:

> *Of voluntary acts we do some by choice, others not by choice; by choice those which we do after deliberation, not by choice those which we do without previous deliberation. Thus there are three kinds of injury in transactions between man and man: those done in ignorance are mistakes. . . . Now when the injury takes place contrary to reasonable expectation, it is a misadventure. When it is not contrary to reasonable expectation, but does not imply vice, it is a mistake (for a man makes a mistake when the fault originates in him, but is the victim of accident when the origin lies outside him). When he acts with knowledge but not after deliberation, it is an act of injustice — e.g. the acts due to anger or to other passions necessary or natural to man; for when men do such harmful and mistaken acts they act unjustly, and the acts are acts of injustice, but this does not imply that the*

doers are unjust or wicked; for the injury is not due to vice. But when a man acts from choice, he is an unjust man and a vicious man. (NE 1135b7–25)

Having the virtue of justice — that is to say, of being fully human — is not, then, simply acting in accordance with the law. It is not a matter of obeying the law out of a desire to *appear* good or out of fear of being punished or of being seen to be guilty if we transgress, but because it is good to act in this way and, even more, because we want others in the city-state to orient themselves towards happiness. The most perfect and, therefore, happiest man is the one who has reached real moral and human maturity. He has integrated the law. He no longer has any difficulty in controlling his passions, nor does he have to battle with them. Instead, he is motivated by the desire that the city-state be a place of peace and its citizens attain true happiness.

The Justice of the Ruler

Now, if we examine the law from the vantage point of the legislators, those who think about and make laws, the virtue of justice is even more necessary. How will laws ever be just if the legislator does not desire justice? Aristotle expands on a whole series of ideas about the qualities required in those who devise laws.

Similarly, those who rule must first submit themselves to the law like any other citizen, for their authority comes from the law and not from what they may want.

This is why we allow only reason, not a human being to be a ruler; for a human being awards himself too many

goods and becomes a tyrant, but a ruler is a guardian of
what is just and hence of what is equal (and so must not
award himself too many goods). (NE 1134a35–b3)[3]

The exercise of power in accordance with justice, with a view to the good of all citizens, is difficult. The exercise of it in one's own interests — for one's own glory, in order to remain in power and have privileges, or to gain money and live by corruption — is of course a great temptation for those in power. When it comes, for example, to the distribution of honours, the temptation to succumb to nepotism and favour one's friends can be great.

It is precisely a quality of a good ruler to be able to distribute "honour or money or the other things that fall to be divided among those who have a share in the constitution" (NE 1130b30) with equity. This sense of equity, which is not strict equality, but proportional — to each according to his merits — springs from distributive justice.

A Superior Sense of Justice

With great finesse, Aristotle also describes a virtue particular to those who rule, or indeed to all citizens who are in some sense above legal or written justice. It is not that the ruler considers himself above the law. On the contrary, he seeks to comply with the spirit of the law, and that is why he authorizes himself not to respect its letter. This virtue of those who rule is called *epieikes*, which is often translated as "equity," but which is not the same thing as the sense of just distribution referred to above. *Epieikes* is a superior form of justice that implies an acute sense of discernment.

This higher virtue of justice comes into play because

the law must always speak universally. It cannot know, provide for, or regulate for every individual situation. This virtue may, therefore, run counter to the written law and hence legal justice. It is nevertheless just, "not the legally just but a correction of legal justice" (NE 1137b11). In this case the law remains correct. "The error is not in the law nor in the legislator but in the nature of the thing" (NE 1137b17). Thus the man who acts in accordance with his conscience is acting in accordance with justice, in the knowledge that the legislator would have done the same if he had been confronted with this particular situation.

> *The equitable* [epieikes] *is just, but not the legally just but a correction of legal justice. The reason is that all law is universal but about some things it is not possible to make a universal statement which shall be correct. . . . When the law speaks universally, then, and a case arises on it which is not covered by the universal statement, then it is right, where the legislator fails us and has erred by over-simplicity, to correct the omission — to say what the legislator himself would have said had he been present.* (NE 1137b11–23)

> *It is plain then, what the equitable* [epieikes] *is, and that it is just and is better than one kind of justice* [written]. *It is evident also from this who the equitable man is; the man who chooses and does such acts, and is no stickler for his rights in a bad sense but tends to take less than his share though he has the law on his side, is equitable.* (NE 1137b33–1138a2)

Clearly this idea of there being an exception to the rule is potentially explosive. Who is going to guarantee that a ruler will not create exceptions to suit his own ends? The same question applies to the person who gives himself dispensation from abiding by the law. It is obvious that this virtue, *epieikes*, can only be exercised by integrated men who desire moral truth. At the same time, it is a virtue that touches on the very substance of moral experience: what is concrete. The law is universal, but action is always particular. Hence there exists the possibility of distortion, but also the opportunity for prudent judgement.

Rectificatory Justice

There is yet another dimension to justice that Aristotle refers to as *rectificatory*, and which consists of re-establishing equality, a role that in the final resort falls to the judge, who must be an embodiment of justice. When one man has stolen from another or destroyed another person's property, people will have recourse to the law. The judge seeks to re-establish equality.

> . . . *for in the case also in which one has received and the other has inflicted a wound, or one has slain and the other been slain, the suffering and the action have been unequally distributed; but the judge tries to equalize things by means of the penalty, taking away from the gain of the assailant. For the term "gain" is applied generally to such cases, even if it be not a term appropriate to certain cases, e.g. to the person who inflicts a wound — and "loss" to the sufferer; at all events when the suffering*

*has been estimated, the one is called loss and the other
gain. Therefore the equal is intermediate between the
greater and the less.* (NE 1132a8–14)

*This is why, when people dispute, they take refuge
in the judge; and to go to the judge is to go to justice; for
the nature of the judge is to be a sort of animate justice;
and they seek the judge as an intermediate, and in some
states they call the judges mediators.* (NE 1132a19–24)

The Highest Virtues on the Moral Plane

As we can see, magnamity and justice are like pinnacles
on the moral plane in the same way that wisdom is on
the intellectual plane. "The magnanimous man is the
best of men" (NE 1123b30); magnanimity seems to be
"a sort of crown of the virtues; for it makes them greater
and it is not found without them" (NE 1124a1). And
"justice is complete virtue" and is often thought to be
"the greatest of virtues" (NE1129b26–29).

If Aristotle takes the wise man and the magnanimous
man to be two men enjoying the most perfect happiness
possible to human beings, is it not because, for him, the
highest good — happiness — is to be desired for its own
sake and not with a view to anything else (NE 1097b14–16)?
Happiness is something self-sufficient, as is the happy
man, within the limits of his nature. Aristotle cannot conceive of a man's happiness being dependent on anything
other than his own choice, aiming at something greater
than himself. The wise man and the magnanimous man
are two examples of this independence.

That happiness stems from within a person is obvious to all. But why does Aristotle provide us with examples that seem so impossible for most freemen to realize? Is it not because for him this is the ultimate, or the most complete, path to total happiness? Not everyone can be wise or magnanimous, but everyone can be aware that human nature is realized when we take the path towards the noblest virtues. Everyone can in some way share in these virtues. To seek to know God with the greatest certitude and to do great things in society, each according to his abilities — therein lies happiness.

CHAPTER 5

THE TIME FOR GROWTH

For Aristotle, the science of ethics is a practical one. It is concerned with helping people to grow in their humanity, to become good, wise, just, and, to put it in a nutshell, happy. Ethics are not merely to be learned about theoretically, but actually to be implemented.

> *Since, then, the present inquiry does not aim at theoretical knowledge like the others (for we are inquiring not in order to know what virtue is, but in order to become good, since otherwise our inquiry would have been of no use), we must examine the nature of actions, namely how we ought to do them.* (NE 1103b26–31)

There is no way of becoming just, wise, and good other than through the actual exercise of these virtues through the daily regulation of our spontaneous desires by the *logos*. "States of character arise out of like activities. This is why the activities we exhibit must be of a certain kind" (NE 1103b20). Temperate action gradually creates the virtue of temperance. In order to become accomplished and mature, a man needs good dispositions, among them good health and a good education. He needs to have opted definitely for a good life and true happiness, and desire to progress towards that end; this involves work on himself, effort and struggle in order to look clearly into himself and orient his passions towards the best goal. Becoming a mature human being takes time.

In this chapter we are going to reflect upon how we may grow in our humanity. How can we bring about that inner state of being, which will make our judgement and choices easy and joyous? How can we progress so that our activities stem from virtue and are not simply driven by our passions?

The Acquisition of Virtue

No progress would be possible if nature did not help us in the first place. It is, after all, by nature that the soul, body, and natural dispositions to think and act exist.

> *This is why these states are thought to be natural endowments — why, while no one is thought to be a philosopher by nature, people are thought to have by nature judgement, understanding and intuitive reason. This is shown by the fact that we think our powers correspond to our time of life, and that a particular age brings with it intuitive reason and judgement; this implies that nature is the cause.* (NE 1143b6–9)

This conception of man is ultimately quite optimistic. There would be no point in working at the virtues if there were not within us a connivance between them and us.

Neither by nature, then, nor contrary to nature do the virtues arise in us; rather we are adapted by nature to receive them, and are made perfect by habit. (NE 1103a23–25)

The Human Soul

To help us understand how man can grow towards full humanity and happiness, Aristotle draws on his vision of the human soul.

Of the irrational element one division seems to be widely distributed, and vegetative in its nature, I mean that which causes nutrition and growth. (NE 1102a28–b1)

There seems to be also another irrational element in the soul — one which in a sense, however, shares in a rational principle. (NE 1102b13)

Aristotle is referring here to the desires for food, drink, and sexual relations that are born spontaneously. In themselves these have no *rational principle*. They need to be permeated with reason in order to be oriented as they should be, towards the end of self-mastery and justice.

And Aristotle adds that in these desires,

. . . the vegetative element in no way shares in a rational principle, but the appetitive, and in general the desiring element in a sense shares in it, in so far as it listens to and obeys it. (NE 1102b31)

Aristotle sees several potencies in the human soul. Some derive from the mind, others from the body, and yet others derive from both. How is food absorbed and how does it make us grow? That is beyond our control. Reason can do nothing about it. The soul assumes control of our vegetative functions without consulting our reason. There is no scope for freedom in this domain: "The vegetative element in no way shares in the rational principle" (NE 1102b29).

The desiring element, on the other hand, which nourishes the passions, is of the body while still being open to the mind. It can pay heed to the *logos*. "There seems to be also another irrational element in the soul — one which in a sense, however, shares in a rational principle" (NE 1102b13). In themselves our desires tend to be chaotic, either excessive or defective. Like runaway, riderless horses, they await direction. Man's proper task is to take hold of the reins and guide them, to orient these desires, with all their fulminating energy, towards the sought-after end. It is a question of opening up the desiring element to the rational principle, to the *logos*, so that it may be imbued with and permeated by the intelligence.

Education and Pleasure

In all this undertaking, education is important. It is education that orients us before we are able to take control of our own growth. It is education that determines our relationship to pleasure.

> *It is on account of the pleasure that we do bad things, and on account of the pain that we abstain from noble ones. Hence we ought to have been brought up in a particular way from our very youth, as Plato says, so as both*

to delight in and to be pained by the things that we ought; for this is the right education. (NE 1104b10–12)

It makes no small difference, then, whether we form habits of one kind or another from our very youth; it makes a very great difference, or rather all the difference. (NE 1103b24–25)

Aristotle provides us with the rules for becoming virtuous. First we must perform virtuous acts. "We become just by doing just acts, temperate by doing temperate acts" (NE 1103b1). It is not a case of remaining in a state of moral awareness but of *doing* acts that lead passion to be submitted to and inspired by reason, so that the passionate energy is directed where it should be. This sometimes involves a struggle, because there are elements in passion that do not want to submit. It is only when the struggle is over and passion has been totally moulded by intelligence that we become truly virtuous.

There is a lot of work to be done when it comes to discriminating between the immediate, sensible pleasures and the highest pleasures. In fact, the desiring element in the soul wants to possess the object it desires; it is driven by impulse towards it. When we are hungry, we experience a desire for food. This desire must be controlled in order to eat what we should, when we should, and how we should. When someone is aggressive towards us, we should not allow ourselves to be carried away by uncontrolled anger. We should master our own aggression.

Hence also it is no easy task to be good. For in everything it is no easy task to find the middle, e.g. to find the middle of a circle is not for every one but for him who knows; so, too, any one can get angry — that is easy — or give or spend money; but to do this to the right person, to the right extent, at the right time, with the right motive, and in the right way, that is not for every one, nor is it easy; wherefore goodness is both rare and laudable and noble.

Hence he who aims at the intermediate must first depart from what is the more contrary to it, as Calypso advises — "Hold the ship out beyond that surf and spray."

For of the extremes one is more erroneous, one less so; therefore since to hit the mean is hard in the extreme, we must as a second best, as people say, take the least of the evils; and this will be done best in the way we describe. (NE 1109a24–35)

In every one of us there is an almost natural tendency that drives us to the extremes of too much or too little, whether in action or desire. To find the happy medium between these two extremes, we have to learn to know ourselves and to guard against the desire that impels us towards one or the other of them.

But we must consider the things towards which we ourselves also are easily carried away; for some of us tend to one thing, some to another; and this will be recognizable from the pleasure and the pain we feel. We must drag ourselves to the contrary extreme; for we shall get into the intermediate state by drawing well away from error, as people do in straightening sticks that are bent. (NE 1109b2–7)

If we know that we have a tendency or that it is a fault

of ours to talk too much about ourselves and be boastful, we should hold our tongue and avoid pushing ourselves to the fore, and speak only when we should, to whom we should, in the way that we should. Similarly, if we know that we are afraid to act, that we lack confidence in ourselves, and that we are pusillanimous, we should strive to move in the opposite direction in order to be truly human. This is judicious advice for anyone wanting to reach maturity as a human being.

> *Now in everything the pleasant or pleasure is most to be guarded against; for we do not judge it impartially.* (NE 1109b8–9)

Another sound piece of advice! But obviously Aristotle is not talking here about all pleasure — because, as we have seen, there is great pleasure to be derived from acts of goodness and justice — but about those forms of pleasure that lure us away from the truth and the golden mean. He goes on:

> *We ought, then, to feel towards pleasure as the elders of the people felt towards Helen, and in all circumstances repeat their saying;[1] for if we dismiss pleasure thus we are less likely to go astray.* (NE 1109b9–11)

From Virtuous Acts to Virtue

It is when a man's passions begin to be subject to and permeated by reason that he becomes virtuous. His life takes on direction. He knows where he is going. He ceases to be a weathervane, swinging about in all directions, shaken by his passions. He is not torn apart by different desires that fragment him and lead him into unjust acts. Then everything that was latent within him develops. Gradually his character becomes stable. He builds an inner unity. He learns how to act and to act as a man. And so he opens himself to others.

All this takes time, for the virtues are not acquired overnight. Many a virtuous act will still be accomplished only with difficulty and after a struggle against opposing desires. The acts may be virtuous, but virtue has not yet been established as an intimate disposition of the soul, ready for action. Only when at last just and true action becomes easy and a source of pleasure, can we be sure that it stems from complete and perfect virtue. For this reason Aristotle tells us that virtue is always associated with pleasure and pain. Truly virtuous action is a source of pleasure. The mark of virtue is thus the pleasure derived from it.

> *We must take as a sign of states of character* [established virtue] *the pleasure or pain that ensues on acts; for the man who abstains from bodily pleasures and delights in this very fact is temperate, while the man who is annoyed at it is self-indulgent, and he who stands his ground against things that are terrible and delights in this or at least is not pained is brave, while the man who is pained is a coward.* (NE 1104b3–8)

Thus Aristotle does not rule out desire. Far from it! For him, it is a question of desiring the things we should, when we should, and how we should. The desiring element is like a vital flow of energy that must be oriented. This orientation is the work of reason. And all this takes time.

It is interesting to note that, for Aristotle, there are different kinds of desires. Let us take first the desires for food, drink, and sexual relations, which must be controlled by reason in order that a man may be master of himself and temperate. There are also fears in him that must be controlled if he is to be courageous and stand his ground in the face of adversity. These are the classic passions. But there are other, more subtle forms of desire, associated with the desire to give thoughtlessly, and not for the other person's good, in order to appear important or court the attention of flattering friends; those linked to the desire for recognition, or to the desire for social success at any price, regardless of all considerations of truth and justice.

Aristotle also speaks of other desires that drive us to avarice or pusillanimity — under the influence of fear or insecurity — which show that we lack self-confidence and are afraid of conflict, that we are hiding and shut in on ourselves. Wanting constantly to give, to give too much, at the wrong time, repeatedly, in defiance of any common sense, typically stems from what is nowadays known as *compulsion*. Today the human sciences have worked out a theory for this. Would it not be worthwhile to look more closely at how these latter forms of desire stem from either the desiring element in the soul or from what is known as "aggression" or "anger"? Aristotle actually tells us that "irrational craving is two fold, viz. anger and appetite" (Rhet. 1369a5).

Knowing How to Choose

Realizing ourselves and orienting ourselves towards human happiness require us to make choices. Deliberate choice, or "purpose," is at the heart both of Aristotelian ethics and of human reality, "for in purpose lies the essential element of virtue" (NE 1163a23). It implies freedom. An act that has really been chosen proceeds from within; it is not forced or constrained by fear or external circumstances. It is a free act.

> *But if our conclusion appears true, and we cannot refer (actions) back to other origins beyond those in ourselves, then it follows that whatever has its origin in us is itself up to us and voluntary.* (NE 1113b19)[2]

The desire for happiness is not subject to choice; it is a natural and spontaneous tendency. Choice occurs when we actively *want* to be happy, and we adopt whatever means we estimate will take us in the direction of happiness. Of course, through weakness or ignorance or by allowing ourselves to be carried away by uncontrolled passions, it is quite possible for us to choose a good that provides only passing pleasure.

For Aristotle, a person constructs himself through the choices that shape his personality, making him a complete (or incomplete) human being. He cannot be moral without the room afforded by freedom. Aristotle notes that slaves do not have the same room for choice and freedom as freemen, or citizens. Because they are subject to authority, slaves cannot choose what is greatest in a human being. But, within their parameters, they can acquire the virtue that is appropriate to them.

Who are the slaves of our time, the people whose freedom is restricted? We may think at once of immigrants or poor people, who often can make no real choices. But let us think too of some company executives, who, because of social or cultural pressure, submit to working much more than they would choose to. They need large salaries to keep up a certain lifestyle or possibly to pay off debts. When they get home at the end of the day, many of these business people are too tired to do anything but watch television; they become subject to the television. At what point do they make real choices?

To attain real human happiness, we need to be responsible for our own lives and to act from free choice in every circumstance: to choose the truth beyond all lies and illusion; to choose what is just, taking the interests of others into account; to choose our good. We should not act solely in our own interests and for our own glory, nor should we refuse to act, out of fear or laziness. And let us not forget that choice involves loss. If we choose a woman or a man to be our wife or husband, we renounce thousands of others! Our lives are shaped by the choices we make. It is by this means that we find our identity. If we choose to work for society — a highly human undertaking in Aristotle's view, because it means acting for the good of others — this implies that we choose the appropriate studies, that we accept guidance and have models, and that we engage progressively in political and social action in order to acquire experience; that we reject corruption, power at any price, and all forms of injustice. All this takes time and effort.

Each of us attributes happiness to different things. That is why we need to take time to reflect and possibly learn about the science of ethics in order to choose *true* human happiness. We must not allow ourselves to be influenced by prevailing values and do "what everyone else does," or allow ourselves to be sidetracked by superficial pleasures or by masters — sophists — whose teaching is a far cry from the truth. Thus it is a case of getting a grip on our own lives, choosing and choosing well, and then remaining true to our choices. Aristotle notes that not only does choice consist of an activity that aims at a certain good, it is also the refusal (the non-choice) of an activity. Not making a choice is still a choice.

For where it is in our power to act it is also in our power not to act, and vice versa. (NE 1113b8)

If there are unruly men who choose intemperance and act contrary to what is just, there are also men whose mastery of themselves is uncertain — they cannot make choices. Some are mentally ill or psychologically weak. They are not capable of introducing reason into their passion; rather their passions control them. Others may lack strength, willpower; they suffer from being too malleable, they easily succumb to temptation. This malleability or weakness of will manifests itself in intemperance and anger and other activities that contravene good behaviour. Then, there are those who are truly perverse or brutish, but fortunately this is rarely found among men, says Aristotle, who with the prejudice of an ancient Greek, adds, "It is found chiefly among barbarians" (NE 1145a30).

Of this latter group, Aristotle cites some horrific examples still found in our day, though possibly in different guises: in Nazi concentration camps, in the Russian gulags, or in of the genocides perpetrated in the former Rwanda and the Balkans.

I mean the brutish states, as in the case of the female, who, they say, rips open pregnant women and devours the infants, or of the things in which some of the tribes about the Black Sea that have gone savage are said to delight — in raw meat or in human flesh . . .

These states are brutish, but others arise as a result of disease (or, in some cases, of madness, as with the man who sacrificed and ate his mother, or with the slave who ate the liver of his fellow), and others are morbid states resulting from custom, e.g. the habit of plucking out the hair or of gnawing the nails, or even coals or earth, and in addition to these paederasty; for these arise in some by nature, and in others, as in those who have been the victims of lust from childhood, from habit. (NE 1148b20–31)

For every excessive state whether of folly, of cowardice, of self-indulgence, or of bad temper, is either brutish or morbid; the man who is by nature apt to fear everything, even the squeak of a mouse, is cowardly with a brutish cowardice, while the man who feared a weasel did so in consequence of disease; and of foolish people those who by nature are thoughtless and live by their senses alone are brutish, like some race of the distant barbarians, while those who are so as a result of disease (e.g. of epilepsy or of madness) are morbid. (NE 1149a5–12)

Prudence

Choice also implies that we can clearly identify, and are capable of grasping in concrete form, the best means of attaining our sought-after end. Aristotle calls this intellectual capacity *phronesis*, or prudence.

In contemporary parlance the prudent man is one who is a little anxious or timid, afraid to make a decision, not daring to take risks. For Aristotle, however, the prudent man knows how to make decisions and take risks in order to reach his desired end. Prudence, in this sense, is a form of practical wisdom, an understanding of life.

> *Now it is thought to be the mark of a man of practical wisdom* [prudence] *to be able to deliberate well about what is good and expedient for himself... about what sort of things conduce to the good life in general.* (NE 1140a25–28)

This virtue enables a man to reach good decisions not only for his own benefit, but also for the benefit of others in society. That is why there is such a thing as political prudence.

> *It is for this reason that we think Pericles and men like him have practical wisdom* [prudence], *viz. because they can see what is good for themselves and what is good for men in general; we consider that those who can do this are good at managing households or states.* (NE 1140b6–11)

Thus prudence is involved in all virtues. The courageous man knows when to go off to fight — it is a matter of practical wisdom — and can assess until what point he should stand his ground. The temperate man knows just what he needs to eat and drink in order not to deviate from his sought-after end. This practical assessment is something that precedes choice. Indeed, once we can see clearly what we should do and how we should do it, we are in a position to make a good choice.

Aristotle notes that "with the presence of the one quality, practical wisdom, will be given all the virtues" (NE 1145a1).

To be happy, one must know not only where one is going, but also how to get there. Some people have a just vision for society and for themselves, but are somewhat cut off from practical reality. They do not know quite how to progress to their end. They are idealists, or at least trapped in their own ideas. They do not know what the first step should be, or do not dare to take it. They lack the virtue of prudence. Others have a good intuition about what they should do, but do not know where it will lead them. They are pragmatists, unaware of the possible or probable consequences of their actions. They have flair, but not the virtue of prudence.

Prudence, in the final reckoning, has a view to the best activity, which stems either from philosophical wisdom or from the virtue of justice.

> But again it is not supreme over philosophic wisdom, i.e. over the superior part of us, any more than the art of medicine is over health; for it does not use it but provides for its coming into being; it issues orders, then, for its sake, but not to it. (NE 1145a6–9)

Such a vision of ethics and humanity might give the impression that Aristotle wants us to be very serious and austere. But although prudence has a view to wisdom, we still remain human beings. It is a question of exercising wisdom and justice in our capacity as people who have families and friends, and who take pleasure in food and good wine; who know how to laugh and make others laugh; who love beauty and everything that is human.

While still emphasizing the intellectual dimension of ethics, Aristotle encourages us to take time to think not only about what we want in life, the goal that we wish to set ourselves, but also about the best means of attaining it.

Is this not why Aristotle describes the magnanimous man as a man who is not stressed? He takes the time to choose well. He does not get bogged down in details. He does not rush to the right or left. He chooses to do what is most important.

Our knowledge of what we want to do with our lives becomes more specific with time, just as it takes time for us to see more clearly the best ways of attaining our end. Becoming a structured, stable, well-oriented person — or, to use Aristotle's word, "virtuous" — takes time. The choices and the prudence will be different in the case of a young person from those of a mature one. It is a question of growing gradually in virtue and in the consciousness we have of our sought-after end, and therefore of happiness.

There are, then, stages to growth.

Some of Aristotle's interpreters place too much emphasis on the happy medium when giving concrete expression to his thought. For them, Aristotle's is an ethical system of balance, along the lines of the inscription at Delphi: "nothing in excess." For an ancient Greek there was nothing worse than lack of moderation. To be accomplished meant being beautiful, not just physically — although corporeal beauty was very important to the Greeks — but also morally. Happiness meant being a "beautiful man" in every sense of the term.

These interpretations are in part true, but tend to overlook a fundamental aspect of Aristotelian ethics, namely that happiness is an *activity* performed with a view to an end. And the greater and more beautiful the activity — as determined by its object — the more intense the happiness. To place too much emphasis on beauty and balance is to risk suggesting that happiness is a narcissistic satisfaction with oneself, as if happiness could be derived from looking at ourselves in a mirror.

A Moral System of Desire and End

A man is accomplished if he acts for the sake of an end that is good. It is always the end, or the intention — the reason why we do something — that makes a man virtuous and happy, or the opposite. Obeying the written law merely in order to impress those about us or to have power cannot be a source of real happiness; it is, quite simply, hypocritical. Nor can being courageous in battle to uphold a tyrant be virtuous and a source of happiness.

Let us remind ourselves of the fundamental principle of the *Ethics*:

> *Every art and every inquiry, and similarly every action and pursuit, is thought to aim at some good.* (NE 1094a1–3)

> *If then, there is some end of the things we do, which we desire for its own sake (everything else being desired for the sake of this) . . . clearly this must be the good and the chief good.* (NE 1094a18–21)

What makes a man good and his activity really human — the source of true happiness — is the ultimate end with a view to which he undertakes this activity.

In all the states of character we have mentioned, as in all other matters, there is a mark to which the man who has the rule looks, and heightens or relaxes his activity accordingly, and there is a standard which determines the mean states which we say are intermediate between excess and defect, being in accordance with the right rule. (NE 1138b18–25)

There are two things in which all well-being consists: one of them is the choice of the right end and aim of action, and the other the discovery of the actions which are means towards it. (Pol. 13331b26–29)

. . . and in actions the final cause is the first principle. (NE 1151a15)

Aristotle provides us with a whole hierarchy of ends, some better than others. And they are attained progressively.

Again, those actions are noble for which the reward is simply honour, or honour more than money. So are those in which a man aims at something desirable for some one else's sake; actions good absolutely, such as those a man does for his country without thinking of himself; actions good in their own nature; actions that are not good simply for the individual. . . . Also all actions done for the sake of others . . . and all successes which benefit others and not oneself. (Rhet. 1366b35–1367a7)

If virtue is a faculty of beneficence, the highest kinds of it must be those which are most useful to others. (Rhet. 1366b4)

> *. . . a bad man seems to do everything for his own sake . . . while the good man acts for honour's sake, and the more so the better he is, and acts for his friend's sake, and sacrifices his own interest.* (NE 1168a32–35)

The accomplished man is thus one who acts in the interests of others in society. On this point Aristotle is clear. In his treatise on friendship he asks himself whether the virtuous man loves himself. Yes, he answers, but not in the same way as the man who is shut in on himself in the pursuit of pleasure. Real self-love is realized by orienting itself towards others. In Chapter 2, on friendship, we have quoted this deeply meaningful text at greater length.[3]

> *It is true of the good man too that he does many acts for the sake of his friends and his country, and if necessary dies for them . . . Rightly then is he thought to be good, since he chooses nobility before all else. But he may even give up actions to his friend; it may be nobler to become the cause of his friend's acting than to act himself.* (NE 1169a17–34)

In his analysis of the moral virtues, we find that Aristotle sees the end as being in the *other*. Justice is a virtue for the other. The virtuous man acts in this way because it is *good*. Through these actions for others he attains his own perfection and the sought-after end that gives a human being unity.

Moral Rectitude
Aristotle often refers to the virtuous man as acting with a

view to moral goodness. Goodness, plain and simple, he calls *agathos*. The moral good or "nobility-and-goodness" is *kalos*.

> *Now goodness [agathos] and nobility-and-goodness [kalos] differ not only in name but also in themselves. For all goods have ends which are to be chosen for their own sake. Of these, we call noble [kalos] those which, existing all of them for their own sake, are praised. For these are those which are the source of praised acts and are themselves praised, such as justice itself and just acts.* (EE 1248b17–22)

The perfectly accomplished man is an honest man of integrity and truth. He does not act in order to have power at any price, to attract attention to himself, to be acclaimed and receive honours, or to shut himself away in self-satisfaction, but because it is just and good to act in such a way. It corresponds with the most profound goodness of his human nature.

The good man is not a super-proud man centred on himself. His perfection resides in the activities through which he honours the divinity by contemplation or in those that are oriented to the good of others.

This ethical vision unifies an apparent contradiction: that of acting for one's own sake (egoism) or acting for the sake of another (altruism). In creating this unity, Aristotle avoids one of life's pitfalls, that of devoting oneself to others to the point of exhaustion. If we are oriented to others, it is in order that they may in turn attain their perfection. How can we desire this perfection for another if we do not desire it for ourselves, and if we exhaust ourselves by giving of ourselves? Orientation towards others must be carried out in accordance with practical wisdom, or prudence.

Reverting to the Law
In Chapter 1, we talked about how Aristotelian ethics were a system of morals based on desire and founded on the desire for happiness inscribed in every human heart. True happiness, however, must be identified and chosen. It must be sought after and selected. Here we come back to a fundamental law of nature. The primary law is that we should reflect, put intelligence into our actions, not allow ourselves to be overrun by our passions, and make choices in pursuit of the good. This law is there within us, however; it is not a particular law.

Similarly, knowing when and how to be angry involves an inner regulation, provided by the *logos*, which becomes moral consciousness. And this inner regulation is what is just and correctly perceived by the *logos* — both for the other person and for the person acting. Anger can be good if its purpose is to re-establish justice and help the other person to live in truth. That is the sought-after end.

The way to happiness is thus to allow ourselves to be guided in all things by the *logos* — the inner light that is in each one of us — that aims at a just and true end. This inner light must be the true light, that is to say, an enlightened state of consciousness dependent on the universal, natural law. "All of these [adultery, theft, murder] and suchlike things imply by their names that they are themselves bad" (NE 1107a11). There is no happy medium for actions such as these.

Aristotle refers to what we might call "moral fault" only in relation to injustice. If I had to pursue this notion of *fault* in his works, I would say that it also means not fully accomplishing one's own humanity. A man who performs actions that are objectively bad is harming not only others but himself, too, like the man who does not actively orient himself towards the pursuit of truth or the good of others in society. He is not a truly good man. His accomplishment and therefore his capacity to do good in society are diminished. He does not bring to others the truth and justice that he might have been able to give them. His failure is thus injurious to others and to the common good of society. Society is rendered less beautiful because of the non-accomplishment of his being.

But to acquire virtue, to develop inner rectitude and an upright conscience, we need not only natural dispositions, a good education, and good practices, but also good laws — in the legal sense — that will constrain young men, in particular, to act in accordance with justice. These laws are the work of the city-state.

Society as a Place Where Men May Become Fully Accomplished

At first glance, Aristotle's ethics appear highly individualistic, in that they are based on each person's desire to be happy, which is realized in a pursuit that, for a small number, culminates in the wonder of contemplation. It would be a mistake to confine oneself to such a view, however. At the very beginning of the *Ethics*, Aristotle states that this science is subordinate to political science, because it is nobler to act in order that a large number may attain happiness than to act only for one's own sake. There is a subtle link between these two sciences. Ethics are oriented towards politics, and politics are oriented towards ethics. Political science must endeavour to create laws, a constitution, and institutions that encourage each citizen to make good choices in order to become, as far as is possible, perfectly accomplished men.

The Family and the Village

Aristotle is a realist. A human being needs a family. He is born of a woman and needs a father. Families gather in groups in villages, which are like an extension of the family. The city-state has quite a different dimension to it. In order to live his life to the full, a human being needs a family but he also needs the city-state. In the family he finds life, his primary education, with his natural dispositions for knowledge, goodness, and justice. In the city-state he finds a form of higher education and the means by which to blossom and develop his potential.

Aristotle adopts an opposite stance to the vision developed by Plato in his *Republic*, of a community life in which men and women all live together and the children belong to everyone. Plato's ideal of the "united city" leads him to disregard the family. Aristotle provides a very pertinent argument in support of the family: It is the base cell for the city. It is true that the family can close in on itself and almost become an end in itself. In such instances, people work in the broader society essentially to feed their family; they take no further interest in the city-state or in works of justice, in order to devote all their energy to the well-being of their family. Like Plato, Aristotle recognizes this as a danger. But in the *Republic,* Plato suppresses the family. Aristotle, by contrast and despite the risks, sees the family as necessary. It is the cradle in which men must prepare themselves to work justly in society. The family is not an impediment to working for justice in the wider world. It does not absorb energies to the point of preventing activities that have a view to the common good. Thanks to the education that it inculcates, the family is ultimately oriented towards this common good. In the city-state, each citizen is responsible for the others.

Family life plays another role that is very beneficial to man: It enables him to grow in his humanity, in his capacity as a husband and father.

> *Between man and wife friendship seems to exist by nature; for man is* [human beings are] *naturally inclined to form couples — even more than to form cities, inasmuch as the household is earlier and more necessary than the city, and reproduction is more common to man with the animals.*
>
> *With the other animals the union extends only to this point but human beings live together not only for the sake of reproduction but also for the various purposes of life; for from the start the functions are divided, and those of man and woman are different; so they help each other by throwing their peculiar gifts into the common stock. It is for these reasons that both utility and pleasure seem to be found in this kind of friendship. But this friendship may be based also on virtue, if the parties are good; for each has its own virtue and they will delight in*

the fact. And children seem to be a bond of union (which is the reason why childless people part more easily); for children are a good common to both and what is common holds them together. (NE 1162a17–27)

As to adultery, let it be held disgraceful, in general, for any man or woman to be found in any way unfaithful when they are married, and called husband and wife. (Pol. 1335b37)

For Aristotle, the family is a vital reality because children are the citizens of tomorrow. For Aristotle, as for Plato, however, there should be neither too many children nor too few. For this reason, Aristotle would like marriage to be subject to regulation, so that any children will be strong, vigorous, and healthy. In his day it was actually thought that children born to young couples would be sickly.

The union of male and female when too young is bad for the procreation of children; in all other animals the offspring of the young are small and ill-developed, and with a tendency to produce female children, and therefore also in man, as is proved by the fact that in those cities in which men and women are accustomed to marry young, the people are small and weak. (Pol. 1335a11)

I scarcely think that we would say the same today! In the same chapter, Aristotle affirms that the ideal age for a man to marry is thirty-seven or possibly slightly younger, and for a woman it is eighteen! (Pol. 1135a30)

The City-State

If the village is an extension of the family, the city-state is a collection of villages:

> *When several villages are united in a single complete community, large enough to be nearly or quite self-sufficing, the state comes into existence, originating in the bare needs of life, and continuing in existence for the sake of a good life.* (Pol. 1252b27–29)

In order to become perfectly accomplished, a human being needs to live in a wider context than that of his family or village. He needs the city-state, in which every citizen develops at an intellectual and human level and is able to accomplish a specific task. Plato had already noted in his *Republic* that rulers, teachers, traders, and soldiers were needed, as were people to make clothes and farm, etc. The city-state is the place where a human being lives and makes use of his capacities.

> *. . . it is evident that the state is a creation of nature, and that man is by nature a political animal. And he who by nature and not by mere accident is without a state, is either a bad man or above humanity; he is like the "tribeless, lawless, hearthless one," whom Homer[4] denounces.* (Pol. 1253a2–4)

Because, says Aristotle,

> *. . . nature, as we often say, makes nothing in vain, and man is the only animal whom she has endowed with the gift of speech. And whereas mere voice is but an indication of pleasure or pain, and is therefore found*

in other animals . . . the power of speech is intended to
set forth the expedient and inexpedient, and therefore
likewise the just and the unjust. (Pol. 1253a12–18)

Indeed, for Aristotle, the individual is genetically anterior to the city-state, but the city-state is anterior to it by
nature, because it is in some way the place in which a
human being can develop and find his perfection.

A social instinct is implanted in all men by nature,
and yet he who founded the state was the greatest of
benefactors. For man, when perfected, is the best of ani-
mals, but, when separated from law and justice, he is
the worst of all. (Pol. 1253a 30–32)

It is useful to note here that, for Aristotle, the city-
state (*polis*) bears no resemblance to our contemporary
societies, countries, or nations. Cities were small urban
republics. Athens, the largest, spread over nearly 1,600
square kilometres, and most others covered no more
than about 110 square kilometres. The "city" was thus
an autonomous entity with a unified culture and religion.[5] Aristotle evokes the idea of Hellenic unity and
favours the notion of a federation of cities. The Greek
nation, he claims, "if it could be formed into one state,
would be able to rule the world" (Pol. 1327b34). This
union was never actually realized. What Aristotle says
about systems of government, however, could be
applied, with very slight differences, to our own political societies.

Politics, then, is the science that seeks to organize the
city-state and give it the best possible constitution so that

it may be well governed. The aim of this government is not just to provide for the material well-being of every citizen and help him to acquire a profession and become perfect in it. It should also help him to develop strength of character and a civic sense, to become just and true by working for greater and nobler things than those found in the family or village. A government that does not help its citizens to develop the virtues of honesty and justice, but allows them to act according to their instincts, risks having its citizens stray into conflicts that are dangerous to the city-state.

> *But a state exists for the sake of a good life, and not for the sake of life only. . . . Nor does a state exist for the sake of alliance and security from injustice, nor yet for the sake of exchange and mutual intercourse.* (Pol. 1280a25–30)

> *. . . virtue must be the care of a state which is truly so called, and not merely enjoys the name: for without this end the community becomes a mere alliance which differs only in place from alliances of which the members live apart; and law is only a convention . . . and has no real power to make the citizens good and just.* (Pol. 1280b5–12)

The conclusion is clear:

> *. . . a state . . . is a community of families and aggregations of families in well-being, for the sake of a perfect and self-sufficing life.* (Pol. 1280b30)

The Unity of the City-State

For a human being to be able to develop his humanity, the city-state must be united and at peace. Of course, as history shows us only too clearly, wars can break out anywhere and sometimes they are civil wars. But if all man's energies are taken up with combat, he will scarcely have time to develop, to grow in knowledge and construct a just state. This question of the city-state's unity was one that was central to Plato's thinking.

Marxism and various forms of fascism also see unity as the supreme norm. Government exists with a view to imposing unity, if necessary by means of secret police. How to govern and impose laws that the government considers necessary and essential for the well-being of citizens and state? If political leaders are convinced they are right, that they are the only ones who know what is good for the city and that those who oppose their vision are rebels, miscreants, or delinquents, they will seek to impose their point of view by force and prevent, at any price, these "miscreants" from disturbing the peace and taking power. Plato's view was that it is dangerous to give individuals too much liberty and different viewpoints too much latitude, because it leaves the door open for all kinds of subversion and perversion.

Aristotle wants unity in the city, but by a different means from Plato. He seeks it by encouraging all citizens to be virtuous, good, and, above all, friends. Plato, in his *Republic* (but not in *Statesman* or *Laws*), was inclined to impose the greatest possible unity. For Aristotle, however, imposing unity on a state was likely to lead to its ruin (Pol. 1261b7–15).

Aristotle requires that citizens be freemen: free to grow to proper autonomy, to become virtuous — in short, to develop a full and happy life.

> *For friendship we believe to be the greatest good of states and the preservative of them against revolutions; neither is there anything which Socrates so greatly lauds as the unity of the state which he and all the world declare to be created by friendship. But the unity which he commends would be like that of the lovers in the* Symposium *who, as Aristophanes says, desire to grow together in the excess of their affection, and from being two to become one, in which case one or both would certainly perish. Whereas in a state having women and children common, love will be watery.* (Pol. 1262b7–16)

So, for Aristotle, the unity of the city-state stems from the fact that man is naturally a political animal who finds his fulfillment in virtue and friendship. In this friendship the other person is considered to be different. This is not the "love" described by Aristophanes, which is fusion. Thus, each citizen is free to grow in virtue, especially the virtues of justice and wisdom. Aristotle's criticism of the idea of having possessions, women, and children in common bears witness to the importance he accords the diversity that forms the union.

On this point Aristotle is realistic. He does not expect every citizen to be so taken with the common good and the idea of having all possessions in common that he no longer needs any property or possessions of his own. There is no doubt that having too much can provoke jealousy and discord. But the good man will not go to extremes in this respect and will not be the cause of conflict. Egoism is the fault not of loving oneself, but of loving oneself to an exaggerated degree.

> *Again, how immeasurably greater is the pleasure, when a man feels a thing to be his own; for surely the love of self is a feeling implanted by nature and not given in vain, although selfishness is rightly censured; this, however, is not the mere love of self, but the love of self in excess, like the miser's love of money; for all, or almost all, men love money and other such objects in a measure.* (Pol. 1263a40–b6)

If the perfectly accomplished man is one who works in the city-state for the good of his friends and of everyone, the city-state and, therefore, its constitution are there to help each citizen freely to become what he is called to be, in accordance with his nature, to be happy through the exercise of the most human and most divine activities. Hence the need for good laws and a constitution that is truly just.

The Need for Laws

Affirming that the role of politics is to encourage citizens to become virtuous and develop their civic sense, Aristotle maintains that laws must oblige them to respect others. He knows that it is impossible to force people to be virtuous and work for the good of society. The person who acts out of fear of punishment is not virtuous, but the law can help him to take a step in the direction of virtue. A man's happiness can stem only from free choice. Good laws are therefore needed to protect individuals from injustice and to constrain those who live by their passions not to act on them. The science of ethics, ethical arguments, and encouragement to lead a good life can be helpful, but they are not enough.

> . . . *while they* [arguments] *seem to have power to encourage and stimulate the generous-minded among our youth, and to make a character which is gently born, and a true lover of what is noble, ready to be possessed by virtue, they are not able to encourage the many to nobility and goodness. For these do not by nature obey the sense of shame, but only fear, and do not abstain from bad acts because of their baseness but through fear of punishment; living by passion they pursue their own pleasures and the means to them, and avoid the opposite pains, and have not even a conception of what is noble and truly pleasant, since they have never tasted it.*
> (NE 1179b6–15)

In order to help those who do not yet have the desire to be really good and generous, constraint — fear of the law and of punishment — is necessary. The law is also there to stimulate the desire to be good and generous. But perhaps its most important function is still to help young men to acquire good habits.

> *But it is hard for someone to be trained correctly for virtue from his youth if he has not been brought up to correct laws, since the many, especially the young, do not find it pleasant to live in a temperate and resistant way. Hence laws must prescribe their upbringing and practices; for they will not find these things painful when they get used to them.* (NE 1179b31–35)[6]

But these young men, on reaching adulthood, will still have need of the law.

> *But it is surely not enough that when they are young they should get the right nurture and attention; since they must, even when they are grown up, practise and be habituated to them, we shall need laws for this as well, and generally speaking to cover the whole of life.* (NE 1179b36–1180a3)

> *This is why some think that legislators ought to stimulate men to virtue and urge them forward by the motive of the noble, on the assumption that those who have been well advanced by the formation of habits will attend to such influences; and that punishments and penalties should be imposed on those who disobey and are of inferior nature, while the incurably bad should be completely banished. A good man (they think), since he lives with his mind fixed on what is noble, will submit to argument, while a bad man, whose desire is for pleasure, is corrected by pain like a beast of burden.* (NE 1180a7–13)

Aristotle is not always very optimistic when it comes to the possibility of helping people to change and become more human!

It is not easy in politics to distinguish laws that are necessary to protect citizens against injustice from those necessary to help people to become upstanding, just, and true. In Aristotle, politics intrudes too much upon the private domain for our modern mentality, for example, when Aristotle would like to control the number of children conceived in a family.

The neglect of this subject [limitation of the population], *which in existing states is so common, is a never-failing cause of poverty among the citizens; and poverty is the parent of revolution and crime.* (Pol. 1265b10)

Similarly, he would like to see a law prohibiting the raising of children with a handicap.

As to the exposure and rearing of children, let there be a law that no deformed child shall live, but that on the ground of an excess in the number of children, if the established customs of the state forbid this (for in our state population has a limit) no child is to be exposed, but when couples have children in excess, let abortion proceed before sense and life have begun; what may or may not be lawfully done in these cases depends on the question of life and sensation. (Pol. 1335b18–27)

The Various Forms of Government

If a man needs to live in the city-state in order to develop his intellectual and moral capacities, the form that government takes will be important. In fact, some forms of government crush their citizens and prevent them from becoming fully human. Other forms of government, however, seek the good of all citizens.

The conclusion is evident: that governments which have regard to the common interest are constituted in accordance with strict principles of justice, and are therefore true forms; but those which regard only the interests of their rulers are all defective and perverted forms, for

*they are despotic whereas a state is a community of
freemen.* (Pol. 1279a17–21)

*The true forms of government, therefore, are those
in which the one, or the few, or the many, govern with
a view to the common interest; but governments which
rule with a view to the private interest, whether of the
one, or of the few, or of the many, are perversions.*
(Pol. 1279a 25–30)

Aristotle specifies three just forms of government: monarchy; aristocracy, that is to say, government by the best; and
politia.[7] Their respective perversions are tyranny, oligarchy,
and democracy.

*For tyranny is a kind of monarchy which has in view
the interest of the monarch only; oligarchy has in view the
interest of the wealthy; democracy, of the needy; none of
them the common good of all.* (Pol. 1279b6–10)

To conclude this chapter on politics and justice, it is
interesting to look at Aristotle's insight into how a tyrant
seeks to maintain his power, for it provides us with clues
by which we may recognize tyranny in our own time. Alas,
modern dictators such as Hitler, Stalin, and those in Latin
America have made ready use of these methods. One of the
ways in which a tyrant conserves power, Aristotle tells us, is to

*. . . lop off those who are too high; he must put to death
men of spirit; he must not allow common meals, clubs,
education, and the like; he must be upon his guard
against anything which is likely to inspire either courage*

or confidence among his subjects; he must prohibit literary assemblies or other meetings for discussion, and he must take every means to prevent people from knowing one another (for acquaintance begets mutual confidence). Further, he must compel all persons staying in the city to appear in public and live at his gates; then he will know what they are doing. . . . A tyrant should also endeavour to know what each of his subjects says or does, and should employ spies. . . . Another art of the tyrant is to sow quarrels among the citizens; friends should be embroiled with friends, the people with the notables, and the rich with one another. Also he should impoverish; he thus provides against the maintenance of a guard by the citizens, and the people, having to keep hard at work, are prevented from conspiring. The Pyramids of Egypt afford an example of this policy. . . . The tyrant is also fond of making war in order that his subjects may have something to do and be always in want of a leader. (Pol. 1313a34–b29)

We can see how politics depends on ethics and ethics depends on politics. A citizen has a view to a city and the city has a view to the citizen. But for this to apply, everyone (or the majority of people) must assume responsibility for their own and others' lives. A good ruler must have not only skills but also political prudence, honesty, and a sense of justice. For citizens to grow in virtue, they need honest and wise rulers and a constitution directed at the common interest. When we read how the tyrant acts in order to maintain his power, we may infer by contrast what a true ruler should do in order that citizens may progress collectively to freedom and a truly happy life. Doesn't what was good for Aristotle's city-state hold true for any human organization?

CHAPTER 6

THE SHORTCOMINGS AND THE VALUE OF ARISTOTELIAN ETHICS

Whenever we try to interpret Aristotle's ethics, we risk doing so according to our own vision and personal values. I can vouch for the fact that some translators have misrepresented Aristotle's thinking by using one word instead of another. If, however, we approach the *Nichomachean Ethics* carefully and rigorously, if we seek to understand them from within, placing them in the context of his thinking and his works as a whole in such a way that they are philosophically consistent, we may manage to grasp what is specific in Aristotelian thought. That is what I have tried to do in the preceding pages.

Establishing the shortcomings in his ethics is much more difficult. To what should we compare them? In relation to what norm should they be viewed? We come back to our personal understanding of ethics. In this chapter I will compare Aristotle's ethics not to Kantian or any other clearly defined philosophical ethics, or to Christian or any

other religiously based ethics, but an essentially philosophical system that could be worked out today, some
2,350 years after Aristotle. Since his time the world has
moved on, thought has moved on, and I would say that
humanity has moved on. Many discoveries have profoundly altered the field of human sciences.

If I had to devise a moral philosophy for our time that
was to be accessible to everyone, I would start with three
affirmations:

- Every human being, regardless of his or her limitations,
  culture, or religion, is important and valuable and
  should be respected.
- The worst ill is disdain of another person, which can
  lead to oppression and the suppression of human life.
- In order to progress towards the fullness of life that is
  inscribed in his or her being, every person, at some
  time or other, needs others.

Every person is sacred, and should therefore be
respected. The origins of this affirmation are long-stand-
ing, but since it was codified in the Universal Declaration
of Human Rights in 1948, it may be said to have become
a universal moral certainty, the starting point for all
human rights, and a reference point for international law.
Most men, and the wise among them, accept it as an
incontrovertible truth. It is true that acts of genocide,
repeated wars, and all kinds of oppression and inequality
trample on this great principle, but still it holds good. The
reaction provoked by war in the Balkans and elsewhere is
a demonstration of this fact. We identified with the men
or women being massacred. The cry "Stop!" went up from

many. The universal consciousness that we are all members of the same human race remains very strong. Another person's life is as precious as mine. Every person has a sacred value.

The question has still to be asked as to what constitutes a person. This is a fundamental moral question in human philosophy. Is a child a person? Is it solely the capacity to reason that defines a person? Are people who have been injured or who are mentally handicapped, who are unable to reason or reflect, persons? We are starting to talk about the rights of people with handicaps. The United Nations itself recognizes their rights. There are also pressing questions in relation to the unborn child. At what point do we become a person? At conception? In the third or fourth month? We say that abortion is the termination of a *pregnancy*; we do not speak about terminating *a human life*. This is shocking. The law condemns infanticide. Why then does it permit abortion? There is an urgent need to specify at what point the embryo becomes a person. But the issue seems to be a non-starter. Governments do not dare to make a pronouncement on the subject.

Aristotle, as we have seen, recommends that we should not bring up deformed children and accepts abortion of the embryo, provided it takes place before there is evidence of development. He wants to limit procreation. The ancient Greeks actually thought that too many births could compromise the balance of the economy.

To me, every child is a person. A person is defined not by his capacity to reason but by his capacity for relationship. I say *capacity* for relationship and not relationship itself, advisedly. One of the l'Arche communities in Africa took in a child who had apparently been raised by animals and then been found in a forest by soldiers. At first glance, the child had nothing human about him and was incapable of having a human relationship. Today, ten years after he was welcomed, Robert — as he is now called — walks and eats unassisted and has happy relationships with others. He is obviously a person. He has become what he was capable of becoming by virtue of the fact that he was conceived of a man and a woman. And he has done so thanks to the presence about him of other human beings who awakened his heart, which was buried in the shadowy recesses of his being.

I could say the same thing about other children with severe psychological and physical handicaps, about apparently depraved men and women, in prison or at large, who have committed horrible crimes. Everyone born of a man and a woman is a person, even if their deepest identity remains concealed beneath serious disturbance and depravity. The possibility always exists for any person to awaken to a life of relationship, however minimal, provided he or she is surrounded by respect and love. In the true story recorded in the book *Dead Man Walking*,[1] Helen Prejean, the author, befriends Matthew Poncelet, the condemned murderer of an adolescent couple, during the period leading up to his execution. When Helen starts to demonstrate the faith she has in him and a relationship develops between them, Matthew is transformed. Far more than impending execution and death, her companionship in the depths of his darkness shows him who he really is in his innermost being.

The Shortcomings of Aristotelian Ethics
Such a concept of what constitutes a person is scarcely that of Aristotle, who affirms that it is the *logos* that defines a human being. On the strength of this, he establishes a whole hierarchy. Only men, and of them, only those who are free and well born, are capable of perfect happiness. Women and slaves can experience a certain happiness because they are capable of a virtuous life within their particular parameters, but they are there to serve the family in some way. Aristotle underlines the importance of the family and therefore of respect for women. As we have seen, he refers to women's virtue and the friendship that is possible with their husbands (NE 1162a24). He also appeals for justice in relation to slaves, because they too are human beings. But for him, women and slaves remain inferior to men. They cannot attain the most complete happiness.

> *So it must necessarily be supposed to be with the moral virtues also; all should partake of them, but only in such manner and degree as is required by each for the fulfillment of his duty. Hence the ruler ought to have moral virtue in perfection, for his function, taken absolutely, demands a master artificer, and rational principle is such an artificer; the subjects, on the other hand, require only that measure of virtue which is proper to each of them. Clearly, then, moral virtue belongs to all of them; but the temperance of a man and of a woman, are not, as Socrates maintained, the same; the courage of a man is shown in commanding, of woman in obeying. And this holds of all other virtues, as will be more clearly seen if we look at them in detail, for those who say generally that*

virtue consists in a good disposition of the soul, or in doing rightly, or the like, only deceive themselves. Far better than such definitions is their mode of speaking, who, like Gorgias, enumerate the virtues. All classes must be deemed to have their special attributes; as the poet says of women, "Silence is a woman's glory," but this is not equally the glory of man. (Pol. 1260a13–30)

It [happiness] *will also on this view be very generally shared; for all who are not maimed as regards their potentiality for virtue may win it by a certain kind of study and a care.* (NE 1099b17–19)

Aristotle also succumbs to actual racism and elitism when he cites Euripides: "'It is meet that Hellenes should rule over barbarians'; as if they thought that the barbarian and the slave were by nature one." (Pol. 1127b23–32). It is not inconceivable that Aristotle's words may have been used to justify slavery or the idea of superiority of one race over another.

The Absence of Heart

This rigid vision of things and of the hierarchy of people derives, it seems to me, from the fact that Aristotle bases the value of human beings on their rational and intellectual capacity alone. That is why he gives no human value to children with severe mental handicaps who seem deprived of reason.[2]

For him, what is essential is the exercise of reason and intelligence that make a greater or lesser degree of autonomy possible, and autonomy draws a man closer to God, or the gods. Friendship, for him, is a pinnacle of human life, a marvellous fruit of virtue. But he is ignorant of the importance of the life of relationship, which exists even before the burgeoning of reason.

He cannot therefore conceive of the supreme value of an encounter between two people of the kind Martin Buber describes in his book *I and Thou*. Friendship between unequals, for example, between a rich person and a poor person, is considered by Aristotle only from a perspective that is almost mercantile. For him, the rich or magnanimous person is happy because he can *give*. *Receiving* implies a lack of autonomy, inferiority. Similarly, a man's virtue is to command, a woman's to obey. Aristotle does not see what they can bring one another, not merely in terms of their capacities, but also in terms of their love. On this basis, a *communion* can develop between them that is the sharing not merely of great and fine activities, beautiful thoughts, and generosity, but also of their shortcomings, their weaknesses, and their affective needs. Happiness then consists not of achieving the greatest possible autonomy, in which we appear strong and capable, but of a sharing of hearts and humility in relation to one another. Thus the child can humanize the man in the same way that a person who is weak and bereft can release the goodness, tenderness, and compassion in him, and thereby help him to discover a new inner unity and communion.

The human sciences teach us that the capacity to love develops in the very first months of a child's life through his relationship with his mother. He needs the experience of a first love that is unconditional. That is the mystery of human beings. This first relationship, of the child with his mother and father, is crucial and forms the basis of subsequent deliberate choices. If the small child is wounded by rejection or the absence of this first love, he is likely to lack self-confidence and have great difficulty in acquiring human virtues in later life. Aristotle could not grasp the role of the parent/child relationship in the development of human beings and human intelligence.

Yet Aristotle is not the father of intellectualism that he has at times been accused of being. He has been reproached for the dryness of his philosophy and people have applauded in contrast the affective dimensions of Eastern and Jewish thought. It is true that Aristotle is seeking to understand the universe, whereas the Jewish people receive their knowledge and laws from the God who loves, watches over, and guides them. So it is that in Judaism, the affective is afforded a certain primacy. To stop short at the discursive intelligence seeking to understand, however, is to misunderstand Aristotle. For him, knowledge begins with astonishment and wonder at the universe and culminates in the wonder, peace, and rest of contemplation, or in works of justice in the city-state. He bases his whole approach on a relationship of trust with the world, a relationship that is almost affective with reality as perceived through the senses. He insists on knowledge and the search for truth, provided they are oriented towards others or towards the divinity. In this way Aristotle differs from those for whom the starting (and the finishing) point is in the consciousness of the subject who is thinking.

For Aristotle it is friendship that opens a definitive door to the heart. Between two friends true love exists. The friend is *another self.* He wants what is good for the other person. Both seek the same values. Together they devote themselves to the pursuit of truth and justice in the city-state. The heart element is present, but friendship implies also that the friend is strong and capable and devotes himself to great things. In this way friendship becomes, as we have seen, a pinnacle of human life.

A Lack of Compassion

Aristotle does not reject affectivity, but he does not consider the heart to be the mainspring of human life and relationship. The fact that he does not afford the heart primacy prevents Aristotle from seeing human evolution as a growth towards greater and more universal justice, justice for every human being. Evolution is neither an ancient Greek concept nor an Aristotelian one. For the Greeks, time was cyclical and could not contain the notion of progress. Kindness and a desire for justice for the weak, the sick, the orphaned, and the poor in general appear to be lacking. With him there is no real compassion. Can we say that, in this respect, he comes close to Nietzsche, who despised the weak and those who treated them kindly? No, even if Aristotle does not call for compassion for the weak, he does affirm that the master should deal justly with his slave.

His model is always the magnanimous, the most perfect man. The magnanimous man does great things in the city-state: He brings about reform, he works for justice. While he does not despise weak people or slaves, he does not waste his time on them. Aristotle could not conceive of the fact that weak people might be able to help a man to become more human, to grow in his humanity. In order to do good, the magnanimous man draws upon his personal virtue.

Aristotle does not work out a morality of compassion. In this respect, his ethics differ fundamentally from the Egyptian religion of 2,800 years ago, which stresses the importance of taking care of the weak,[3] and the Jewish religion, which stresses the importance of looking after widows, orphans, and immigrants (see Deuteronomy 10, 17–19). In the time of Isaiah, God revealed what behaviour pleased him: It was not first and foremost the sacrificing of animals in the temple or fasting, but working for the hungry, the poor, and the weak (Isaiah 58). And, in the jubilee year, slaves were to be set free (Leviticus 25).

Religions that afford compassion a place allow for an important human experience. Through relationship with the poor or weak person or with the child, the heart, compassion, and goodness are awakened, and a new inner unity is established between body and soul. It is as if the tension between the intelligence and the body finds a mysterious resolution in the experience of being present to the poor. Compassion engages the body and it is through the body that we draw nearer to others. We discover that the fragile person can help us to accept ourselves with our own frailties and we undergo an inner transformation. We become more human, more welcoming, and more open to others. Aristotle was enclosed behind city walls, the walls of the small world of Greek freemen. How was he to imagine what it was like to be open to others, and to non-Greeks in particular?

Why does Aristotle glorify the intelligence and the capacity for command in freemen and refuse to recognize the same potential in the intelligence of women, slaves, and barbarians? Is this just a problem of culture, or is there something more profound that Aristotle did not or could not grasp?

A Static Vision
As noted above, it seems to me that the desire for order, or the primacy of order over disorder, prevents Aristotle from perceiving the value and importance of every human being. Aristotle is set in a vision that is static and circular.

By contrast, the biblical vision is evolutionary. Time becomes linear. People have a history. They walk beneath God's gaze and expect the fulfillment of the promise He has made them. These people are focused on the future. The Aristotelian vision is very different. It is determined by the nature of each thing. The world and the stars are eternal; living things, plants, and animals are also eternal, not as individuals, but as species. And over and above everything is the Prime Unmoved Mover, pure Action or Energy, the Sovereign Good that is eternal and completely autonomous. In the world, everything has its nature and must be as fully accomplished as possible. The seed most reach its end and bear fruit. A man must be himself, a woman herself, and so must the slave. Each must recognize and respect the place in which nature has put him, and there discover his happiness. In this way each finds his perfection in himself and within the whole of which he is part. Being in his service, a woman and a slave may in some way partici-pate in the good of the man who contemplates or attends to the city-state. One can see similar elements in the caste system in India.

Woe betide anyone who disrupts this order, for he brings disorder to society. If we leave room for the heart, to the point of becoming concerned about a poor person, of wanting him to progress, we upset this order. Those who are in power and rich will lose out. The heart sees farther than intelligence and order, in a way that Aristotle cannot imagine. His vision of order implies that everything must be in its place and capable of being grasped by the *logos*. Disorder eludes the *logos* and risks engendering chaos. Aristotle is a long way from having a sense of history, be it the history of a people or of individuals. He studied closely the evolution of constitutions in the various city-states and the factors that triggered revolutions, but he seems to have been incapable of identifying a much deeper evolution in each person and in the whole of humanity, an evolution that seems obvious to those of us living on the earth at the dawn of the third millennium.

This desire for order, with its static dimension, leads Aristotle at times to grant the rulers of the city-state too much authority. He was a harsh critic of Plato's idealism, or ideology, which inclined towards absolute unity in the city and thereby to total independence and autarchy, suppressing the family. But doesn't Aristotle fall into the same kind of trap when he wants to control the sex lives and birthrate of citizens in order to prevent the population from increasing?

Aristotle wanted legislators to make good laws that would orient and encourage each citizen to be virtuous and therefore happy, but at the same time he insisted that the choice of virtue must be free and unconstrained! How can these two points of view be reconciled? Poorly interpreted, Aristotle's politics could lead to a form of fascism that would *oblige* people to be happy! Similarly, why does he want to give the man greater authority in the family? Is it not to maintain order? How would he see it if women were to start reacting against unjust husbands?

Aristotle's political vision includes some very just elements when it comes to the intervention of governments in the lives of citizens — especially when these rulers have a sense of the human and of the final end of man. Is it not the objective of rulers to lead each citizen towards a happy life, that is to say, a life in accordance with virtue? The state should therefore be concerned with education. After all, if all citizens lapse into intemperance — if they are lax, violent, and selfish, closed in upon themselves, refusing to take an interest in others — the unity of the city is likely to disintegrate. What happens to the city if its citizens are not educated to have a civic sense, and have no desire to work for justice, to conduct themselves as men of integrity who seek to live in truth and avoid all forms of corruption? Would our Western society not benefit from reflecting further upon this point? If education has as its only goal personal success and individual interest, and not the common good, is it not likely that social conflict will increase and society disintegrate? Similarly, if, consciously or unconsciously, laws weaken the essential unit of society, the family, is there not a danger of seeing the rise of citizens without any inner structure, who are incapable of working for justice?

In this order-based morality, we might also ask ourselves how we recognize order. Is it something immutable? For Aristotle, order is manifested in nature and by nature. But is it possible philosophically to know the order of the universe, to discover the reason for this universe? What is its final good? Towards what is it moving? The naïve and simplistic answers of the beginning of the twentieth century — about humanity evolving towards a better life in which there would be no more wars and in which everyone would have what they needed — have been powerfully undermined. Today this vision is obsolete. Humanity has been reduced to ever greater despair by conflicts, oppression, inequality, and genocide. It has lost sight of the meaning of existence. It no longer knows where it is going. Is there in fact any meaning to history and evolution?

The desire for order and the fear of disorder often manifest themselves when new ideas or a new vision appear from within the group or from human society. Those in a position of authority then feel threatened and are tempted to lock the system in place. They think they know what works well and want to hold on to power in order to prevent general disorder. Their certainty prevents the birth of new ideas.

Aristotle's ethics are order-based because they are nature-based, a notion disparaged by modern thinking. Aristotle has faith in nature, which inscribes the law in the heart of all things and all creatures. The seed of a tomato is intended to produce tomatoes. That is the law inscribed in the seed. By the same token, Aristotle seeks the "natural law" of man, that end or action for which his nature prescribes him, in order that he may choose it freely. Modern thinking has totally rejected this notion of natural law, especially in the field of ethics. Like the Sophists of former times, it maintains that the primary natural law is the law of the fittest. Thus it places *nature* and *culture* or *nature* and *freedom* in opposition to one another. Man is on the same side as culture and freedom; he is outside nature and its laws. This strengthening of the opposition of *nature/culture* or *nature/freedom* prevents us from appreciating that human beings also have their nature; that something is inscribed in their being: the movement towards fullness of life.

We find ourselves confronted, therefore, with rigorously opposing concepts of life and ethics. For some, in order to find the truth of our being we must follow the deepest desires inscribed within us. In the final analysis, opposition to this law is suicide for humanity. Modern ecology presents a powerful analogy. The way we are treating nature is causing disasters: air pollution, the greenhouse effect, the annihilation of numerous species of animals and plants. In short, if we take no note of the laws of nature, the laws of our body and mind, we cause a dangerous lack of order in ourselves, in the universe, on the earth, and in society. At the opposite extreme to this morality of nature and order we find the desire to experience unconstrained freedom and omnipotence, to obey no law except our own desires. A person's value is thus manifested by breaking free of all laws and customs, and so expressing creative freedom.

The notion of nature in Aristotle is conducive to a certain humility. Man has received his nature. He has not created it himself. If, therefore, we are to attain fullness of life, it is a matter of listening to this nature. Of course, it is easy to criticize Aristotle when he propounds ideas on nature that are rooted in his time: that children are born sickly, for example, because their parents are too young! But this does not justify rejection of all his ethics. We should not dismiss his notion of a natural law, but, rather, deepen it. What stems from nature and what is the result of culture, of education, or even of our fears and prejudices? Who are the wise men of our day whom we might consult on this question?

It is true that Aristotle teaches ethics intended for an elite. Manual labourers and slaves, as well as women, had, in his eyes, neither the leisure nor the capacity to live in accordance with the greatest virtues. Because of this, his moral science is directed primarily at freemen who live in a certain comfort, who have the time and the means to make choices. Those who cannot make choices, because of their poverty and their position in life, are not party to complete happiness. They survive rather than live. Is this not the plight of many in an era like ours, when there is so much inequality?

There are certainly some important shortcomings to Aristotle's ethics. In giving priority to order, he was unable to afford every human being radical value. It is the message of Jesus, as described in the Gospels, that grants every person — rich, poor, or underprivileged, Jew or Greek — this absolute value. Jesus opened the way to new horizons and to a sense of human evolution moving towards the unity of the human race.

Even though Aristotelian ethics have their limitations, they nevertheless set down some essential principles. They call upon each one of us to use our intelligence to reflect upon what we are and what we could become, and not to allow ourselves to be guided by illusions, dreams, or sophisms — by what everyone else does and says — but to seek the truth about humanity. Ethical reflection is essential. Human beings are not simply assemblies of predetermined or completely chaotic desires. With help, we are capable of taking hold of our lives, of being responsible for our own lives and making choices. Ethics call upon us to become more aware of ourselves and our fundamental motivation. They invite us to ask ourselves what we want out of life and what we are looking for, in order then to orient ourselves with greater truth towards the good that we are capable of choosing, and the happiness we are capable of attaining.

The Value of Aristotelian Ethics

Aristotelian ethics are realistic. They stem from what is human and come back to what is human. On the one hand, Aristotle knows that most men allow themselves to be led by their passions; on the other, he recognizes the grandeur of man, who is specifically different from the animals.

Man is a being who endlessly seeks the keys to happiness. Frequently he stops at mirages, believing he has found the ultimate sources of happiness and healing, only to discover that they are just illusions. So he sets out again on his interminable quest. From generation to generation, human beings have sought to quench their thirst for the limitless: the search for God, the search for the infinite in nature and the heavens, the search for the infinite in love, the search for omnipotence. Human beings cannot stop the quest that so torments them because, if they are conscious of their being, they are also conscious of not being masters of their own destiny. Accidents, illness, the death of those near to us and the prospect of our own death, wars, man's hatred, storms, earthquakes — all go to show that we are not masters of our own future. The universe and its forces are beyond our control. We are but small, mortal fragments in the vast whole. We exist, but we do not have within us all the resources to be fully alive and live forever. That is our tragedy.

Aristotelian ethics do not then rely on a fully developed theory, but on the *desire* in every human being to be happy. Just as a seed planted in the earth will grow to fullness of life, provided it is watered, so a human being aspires to his own fullness of life. The difference between plants and human beings is that the seed, provided it is nourished, will unfailingly spring up and bear fruit, that is to say, it will reach its fullness of life. The human being, for his part, can attain his only through knowledge, choices, and even struggle. This involves, for Aristotle, education and good laws. Man is capable of correctly orienting his life towards happiness, but he is also capable of going astray under the impetus of his passions, which orient him towards false happiness.

We can see then the necessity for a moral science as a science of man — different from psychology — that seeks to clarify the nature of happiness. Knowledge alone cannot make for happiness, insists Aristotle, telling us that there is no point in studying ethics if we are not resolved to seek happiness actively.

Not only does Aristotle base his ethics on the desire for happiness, but the ethics themselves are developed by constantly resorting to the sayings of the many, or at least of the wisest of them, and this is acknowledged. In order to know what is man and a fully lived life, let us ask men. Therein lies Aristotle's wisdom and his realism. In order to understand man, let us listen to man.

Aristotle in fact tells us that there are men, of "superhuman virtue, a heroic and divine kind of nature" (NE 1145a20). They have immersed themselves in the quest for the divine and for justice on earth. In our time, we may think of Mahatma Gandhi, Nelson Mandela, Mother Teresa, the Dalai Lama, Aung San Suu Kyi, or John Paul II. Recognized by many for the eminence of their vision, their goodness, their courage, and their pursuit of justice and truth, they have opened doors to new dimensions in our modern world. They have given history meaning. Sadly, we have also known men as brutish and perverse as Hitler and Stalin, and other men and women who abuse children, push drugs, or kill without reason, simply for the pleasure of killing. Today, as yesterday, poor people and migrants (slaves to work) have little opportunity to make choices. They seek only to survive. We are witnesses to a great divide between people, created by the difference in their capacities on every level. There are the gifted, the exceptionally gifted, and those who are not gifted at all. Each in his or her own way could learn a little from Aristotle's ethics, for in every case it is a matter of emerging a little from shadows, confusion, illusion, and selfishness, and progressing towards a little more light, justice, and truth — a matter of caring for another person, the members of one's family, one's work colleagues, one's neighbours; of being open to others in society and working for them. Aristotle notes to good effect the fact that a poor person can be more generous than a rich person if, in giving little, they give more in proportion to what they possess. The important thing is not the quantity but each person's intention and possibilities.

Aristotle is able to see popular religion as an ally of his

ethics, in that both tend towards the same end: human beings becoming more fully human. He is not blind to the faults in religion, which can obscure a divine reality beneath superstitious elements and encourage men to be centred solely upon themselves. He does not, however, seek to destroy that religion, but rather to purify it, because he sees it as an aid for most men. It can help them to emerge from the darkness of violence, hatred, brutality, and all forms of injustice. Aristotle is a wise man. He seeks to reinforce all the positive energies that might help the men of his time to become more human, more just, more open to others, and, by virtue of this very fact, to be happier, or to rediscover the fact that they were made for happiness.

NOTES

Introduction

1 *Le bonheur, principe et fin de la morale aristotélicienne*
(Happiness as principle and end of Aristotelian ethics).
This book is out of print but may be consulted
in libraries specializing in philosophy.

2 W. D. Ross, *The Basic Works of Aristotle* (New York: R.
Mckeon, 1951).

3 T. Irwin, *Nichomachean Ethics* (Indianapolis: Hackett,
1985).

4 M. Pakulak, *Aristotle: Nichomachean Ethics* Books 8 and 9
(Oxford: Clarendon Press, 1998).

Chapter 1

1 See J. Tricot's note on this point: "*Orexis* is desire, a generic
term of which *epithumia, thumos* and *boulesis* are forms.
Epithumia is the irrational appetite; . . . *thumos* is courage;
. . . *boulesis* refers to the voluntary, rational, reasoned wish
or desire." Aristotle, *Éthique à Nicomaque* (Paris: Vrin,
1979), 31.

2 In Aristotle, virtue is a stable disposition of a human being and a constituent of happiness (see p. 19 of this chapter).

3 Note on NE 1095a10, translated by W. D. Ross, *The Basic Works of Aristotle* (Oxford: Oxford University Press, 1954).

4 J. Maritain, *La Philosophie morale* (Paris: Gallimard, 1960), 59.

Chapter 2

1 See A.-J. Festugière, *Epicure et ses dieux* (Epicurus and his gods) (Paris: PUF, 1997), 46, 47.

2 A Persian king said to have led a life of debauchery.

3 J.-C. Guillebaud, *La Tyrannie du plaisir* (The tyranny of pleasure) (Paris: Seuil, 1998), 116-119.

4 Pent-up anger and frustration over poverty, unemployment, and the conservative government of General Charles de Gaulle gave rise to a mass movement for sweeping social change in France. In May 1968, workers and students took to the Paris streets in an unprecedented wave of strikes, walkouts, and demonstrations.

5 T. Irwin, *Nichomachean Ethics*.

6 Cicero, *Dialogue on Friendship* Vol. XIII (Paris: Les Belles Lettres, 1928), 27.

7 For Aristotle this means that man lives and works in the "city-state" or what we would today call "society."

8 M. de Montaigne, *Essai de l'amitié* (Paris: Gallimard, 1950), 218–232.

9 M. Pakulak, *Aristotle: Nichomachean Ethics*.

10 A. de Saint-Exupéry, *Citadelle* (Paris: Gallimard, 1948).

11 M. de Montaigne, *Oeuvres complètes* Vol. III (Paris: Editions du Seuil, 1967), 398.

12 Aristotle uses a word that cannot be concisely translated but which implies a form of virtue that is excellence.

13 A. de Saint-Exupéry, *Le Petit prince* (Paris: Gallimard, 1999), 72-73.

14 Cicero, *Dialogue sur l'amitié* (Dialogue on friendship) Vol. IV (Paris: Les Belles Lettres, 1928), 10.

15 In the Greek mentality, and in Aristotle's, men and women are not equal in either status or rights. See Chapter 6, "The Shortcomings and the Value of Aristotelian Ethics."

Chapter 3

1 H. Bergson, *La Pensée et le Mouvant*, in *Oeuvres*, (Paris: PUF, 1959), 1454.

2 K. Jaspers, *Introduction à la philosophie* (An introduction to philosophy) Vol. X (Paris: Editions Plon, 1965).

3 The author is here referring to certain strange, ecstatic experiences undergone in the temples of ancient Greece.

4 A.-J. Festugière, *L'Idéal religieux des Grecs et l'Évangile* (The religious ideal of the Greeks and the Gospel) (Paris: Gablada, 1932), 39, 40.

5 Plato records Socrates' words in his *Apology* and these words specifically in passages 21e–30b.

6 R. A. Gauthier, *Commentaire sur l'Éthique à Nichomaque*, Vol. II (Paris: Louvian, 1959), 860.

7 *Eudemian Ethics*, translated by J. Solomon in *The Complete Works of Aristotle*, revised Oxford translation, edited by Jonathan Barnes, Vol. II (Princeton, NJ: Princeton University Press, 1968). See also note 2, Chapter 6.

8 *The Jerusalem Bible* (London: Darton, Longman and Todd, 1968).

Chapter 4

1   "Magnanimity" is translated by W. D. Ross as "pride."

2   See E. Barker, *The Politics of Aristotle* (London: Oxford University Press, 1952), xxiii.

3   T. Irwin, *Nicomachean Ethics.*

Chapter 5

1   "'Who on earth,' they asked one another, 'could blame the Trojan and Achaean men-at-arms for suffering so long for such a woman's sake? Indeed, she is the very image of an immortal goddess. All the same, and lovely as she is, let her sail home and not stay here to vex us and our children after us.'" *The Iliad* Book 3, trans. E. V. Rieu (Middlesex, U.K.: Penguin), 68.

2   T. Irwin, *Nichomachean Ethics.*

3   See page 75.

4   *The Iliad* Book 9, 63.

5   See E. Barker, *The Politics of Aristotle*, 57, note 1.

6   T. Irwin, *Nichomachean Ethics.*

7   What we would now call democracy is what Aristotle calls *politia*: government by all the citizens. For Aristotle, democracy is a perversion of *politia*. It is government by those without material power for the exclusive good of their class and not in the common interest. It is tyranny by the indigent class.

Chapter 6

1 Random House: New York and Toronto, 1993

2 In the *Eudemian Ethics*, already cited on page 106 however, he opens up the possiblity for people without reason to attain truths (EE1248a25b6). Of course Aristotle is not here referring specifically to people with intellectual disabilities, but possibly to those whom the ancient Greeks called "fools" and "prophets."

3 See X. Le Pichon, *Aux racines de l'homme* (Paris: Presses de la Renaissance, 1997), 133, which cites Anemenope: "God prefers the one who honours the poor man to the one who praises the powerful of this world to the heavens."

ACKNOWLEDGEMENTS

This book was written with the collaboration of Élise Corsini, who brought her great skills to both its preparation and its editing. Our discussions about Aristotle enabled us to discover together how Aristotelian ethics might be presented to today's lovers of truth. I am most grateful to her.

I would also like to express my gratitude to Ronan Sharkey, a philosopher friend, whose excellent suggestions enabled me to elaborate more deeply on certain themes.